EXCEL 2021

A Complete Step-by-Step Illustrative Guide from Beginner to Expert. Master the Essential Functions and Formulas in Less Than 20 Minutes a Day. Includes Tips & Tricks

Larry Brown

TABLE OF CONTENTS

INTRODUCTION TO MICROSOFT EXCEL

Microsoft Excel, spreadsheet application launched in 1985 by the Microsoft Corporation. Excel is a popular spreadsheet system, which organizes data in columns and rows that can be manipulated through formulas that allow the software to perform mathematical functions on the data.

Lotus 1-2-3, first sold by the Lotus Development Corporation in 1982, dominated the mid-1980s spreadsheet market for personal computers (PCs) that ran MS-DOS, an operating system sold by Microsoft. Microsoft developed a competing spreadsheet, and the first version of Excel was released in 1985 for Apple Inc.'s Macintosh computer.

Featuring strong graphics and fast processing, the new application quickly became popular. Lotus 1-2-3 was not available for the Macintosh, which allowed Excel to gain a following among Macintosh users. The next version of Excel, and the first version to run on Microsoft's new Windows operating system, followed in 1987. With a graphics-heavy interface designed to run on the latest Windows computers, the powerful program became popular. Lotus was slow to release a Windows version of its spreadsheet, allowing Excel to increase its market share and eventually become the dominant spreadsheet application in the mid-1990s.

Later versions of Excel featured significant upgrades such as toolbars, outlining, drawing, 3-D charts, numerous shortcuts, and more automated features. In 1995 Microsoft changed Excel's naming system to emphasize the primary year of the product's release. Excel 95 was designed for the latest 32-bit computers that used the Intel Corporation's 386 microprocessor.

New editions appeared in 1997 (Excel 97) and 1999 (Excel 2000). In 2003, Excel 2002 was released as part of the Office XP suite and included a significant new feature that allowed users to recover Excel data in the event of a computer crash.

In addition, Microsoft Excel can help us in a single cell to create data. A Microsoft Excel 2010 is a new feature with sparklines. We can quickly notice patterns in the data and can create small charts in a single cell. It's an easy and quick way to highlight all the significance. For example, Microsoft Excel saves our time, seasonal increases or decreases.

Apart from that Microsoft Excel 2010 can quickly use the right data points in zero. For the PivotTables Excel, 2010 can deliver a new exciting filter enhancement. The PivotTables can provide a rich visualization with the Slicer. The PivotTable can help us so can easily filter the data and dynamically segment to display precisely what we need. With the new research, we can spend a little time sifting through large data sets in the PivotTable views and table, and more time analyzing.

Moreover, we can use Microsoft Excel is easily working together such as share, connect, and accomplish. Microsoft Excel Web App in the different locations can make it possible for us to edit the same spreadsheet with others. In the workbooks, they can make and with the number of editors shown in the status bar. We can always know who is editing the workbook with us.

Apart from that, in our data presentations, we can add more sophistication. Excel 2010 gives us easily to improve data bars, more control over styles and icons, and in a few clicks abilities to highlight specific or important items. The negative values also can be displayed in data bars and to more accurately illustrate in the data visuals.

Furthermore, Microsoft Excel 2010 can help us do things become faster and easier. The traditional can be replaced by the new Microsoft Office Backstage such as share. Print, menu to let us save and publish your spreadsheets with just a few clicks. With the improved Ribbons, we can access our favorite commands and become more quickly though by customing tabs. In our work style can help us create our personal experience.

On top of that, the harness is more power to build bigger and more complex spreadsheets with Microsoft Excel 2010. We can easier to analyze and a massive amount of information with the new 54-bit version of Excel 2010. We can analyze large and complex datasets greater than the 2-gigabyte file size of the previous Excel versions.

In a nutshell, we can through Excel Services to publish and share. The SharePoint Server 2010 and Excel Services integration and let the businessman user share analysis and the result across their organization through by publishing spreadsheets for the Web. We can share sensitive business information and business intelligence. For instance, co-workers, business partners in a security-enhanced environment, and business partners.

Make Fast, Effective Comparisons

Excel 2010 delivers powerful new features and tools to help you discover patterns or trends that can lead to more informed decisions and improve your ability to analyze large data sets.

- Get a visual summary of your data using tiny charts that fit within a cell alongside your text data with new Sparklines.
- Quickly, intuitively filter large amounts of information using new Slicer functionality and enhance your PivotTable and PivotChart visual analysis.

Get Powerful Analysis From Your Desktop

The refinements and performance improvements in Excel 2010 make it easier and faster for you to accomplish your work.

- Use the new Search Filter to quickly narrow down the available filter options in your tables, PivotTable, and PivotChart views. Find exactly what you are looking for from up to a million or more items, instantly.
- PowerPivot for Excel 2010, a free add-in, lets you experience fast manipulation of large data sets (often in millions of rows) and streamlined data integration. And you can effortlessly share your analysis through SharePoint Server 2010.
- Work with massive amounts of information more than 2 gigabytes and maximize new and existing hardware investments by using the 64-bit version of Office 2010.

Save Time, Simplify Your Work, And Increase Your Productivity

It's much easier to create and manage your workbooks when you can work the way you want to work.

- Recover unsaved versions of files that you closed without saving! That's right. The version recovery feature is just one of many new features available from the new Microsoft Office Backstage™ view. The Backstage view replaces the traditional File menu in all Office 2010 applications to provide a centralized, organized space for all workbook management tasks.
- Easily customize the improved Ribbon to make the commands you need most accessible. Create custom tabs or even customize built-in tabs. With Excel 2010, you're in control.

Break Down Barriers And Work Together In New Ways

Excel 2010 offers easy ways to enable people to work together on workbooks, improving the quality of their work. Best of all, those with previous versions of Excel can still participate seamlessly.

- You can now work with other people simultaneously on the same workbook in almost any Web browser using Excel Web App.
- Corporate users in companies running SharePoint Foundation 2010 can use this functionality within their firewall.

- If you're in a small company or working on your own, all you need is a free Windows Live ID to simultaneously author workbooks with others.
- SharePoint Excel Services lets you share your easy-to-read workbooks in a Web browser with your team while maintaining a single version of the workbook.

Access Your Workbooks Anytime, Anywhere

Get the information you need, when and how you want it. Now you can easily access your workbooks by taking the Excel experience with you and staying on top of your needs while you're on the go.

1. **Microsoft Excel Web App:** Edit virtually anywhere. View and edit your workbooks in a Web browser when you're away from home, school, or your office.

2. **Microsoft Excel Mobile:** Quickly update and recalculate Excel workbooks. View entire spreadsheets, including charts and formatting. Sort and filter lists or update your data and formulas and instantly see the results with Excel Mobile on your Windows Phone 7 device.

Whether you're working on your budget or travel expenses, collaborating with a team on school or work projects even if your workbooks exceed a million rows Excel 2010 makes it easier to get what you need to be done quickly, with more flexibility, and with better results.

CHAPTER 1: WHAT IS MICROSOFT EXCEL

What Is Excel?

Microsoft Excel is a helpful and powerful program for data analysis and documentation. It is a spreadsheet program, which contains several columns and rows, where each intersection of a column and a row is a "cell." Each cell contains one point of data or one piece of information. By organizing the information in this way, you can make information easier to find, and automatically draw information from changing data.

Excel is a spreadsheet application developed and published by Microsoft. It is part of the Microsoft Office suite of productivity software. Unlike a word processor, such as Microsoft Word, Excel organizes data. in columns and rows. Rows and columns intersect at a space called a cell. Each cell contains data, such as text, a numerical value, or a formula.

Excel Overview

Excel is a tool for organizing and performing calculations on data. It can analyze data, calculate statistics, generate pivot tables, and represent data as charts or graphs.

For example, you could create an Excel spreadsheet that calculates a monthly budget, tracks associated expenses, and interactively sorts the data by criteria.

Below is an example of Microsoft Excel with each of its major sections highlighted. See the formula bar, cell, column, row, or sheet tab links for further information about each of these sections.

What Is Microsoft Excel?

Microsoft Excel is a spreadsheet program used to record and analyze numerical and statistical data. Microsoft Excel provides multiple features to perform various operations like calculations, pivot tables, graph tools, macro programming, etc. It is compatible with multiple ora like Windows, macOS, Android, and iOS.

An Excel spreadsheet can be understood as a collection of columns and rows that form a table. Alphabetical letters are usually assigned to columns, and numbers are usually assigned to rows. The point where a column and a row meet is called a cell. The address of a cell is given by the letter representing the column and the number representing a row.

Why Should I Learn Microsoft Excel?

We all deal with numbers in one way or the other. We all have daily expenses which we pay for from the monthly income that we earn. For one to spend wisely, they will need to know their income vs.

expenditure. Microsoft Excel comes in handy when we want to record, analyze and store such numeric data. Let's illustrate this using the following image.

Excel Basics

If you're just starting with Excel, there are a few basic commands that we suggest you become familiar with. These are things like:

- Creating a new spreadsheet from scratch.
- Executing basic computations like adding, subtracting, multiplying, and dividing.
- Writing and formatting column text and titles.
- Using Excel's auto-fill features.
- Adding or deleting single columns, rows, and spreadsheets. Below, we'll get into how to add things like multiple columns and rows.
- Keeping column and row titles visible as you scroll past them in a spreadsheet, so that you know what data you're filling as you move further down the document.

Documents You Can Create In Excel

Not sure how you can use Excel in your team? Here is a list of documents you can create:

1. **Income Statements:** You can use an Excel spreadsheet to track a company's sales activity and financial health.

2. **Balance Sheets:** Balance sheets are among the most common types of documents you can create with Excel. It allows you to get a holistic view of a company's financial standing.

3. **Calendar:** You can easily create a spreadsheet monthly calendar to track events or other date-sensitive information.

Here are some documents you can create specifically for marketers.

1. **Marketing Budgets:** Excel is a strong budget-keeping tool. You can create and track marketing budgets, as well as spending, using Excel.

2. **Marketing Reports:** If you don't use a marketing tool such as Marketing Hub, you might find yourself in need of a dashboard with all of your reports. Excel is an excellent tool to create marketing reports.

3. **Editorial Calendars:** You can create editorial calendars in Excel. The tab format makes it extremely easy to track your content creation efforts for custom time ranges.

4. **Traffic And Leads Calculator:** Because of its strong computational powers, Excel is an excellent tool to create all sorts of calculators including one for tracking leads and traffic.

This is only a small sampling of the types of marketing and business documents you can create in Excel. In the spirit of working more efficiently and avoiding tedious, manual work, here are a few Excel formulas and functions you'll need to know.

Where Do You Find Or Start Excel?

If you have Excel or the entire Microsoft Office package installed on your Windows computer, you can find Excel in the Start menu.

Keep in mind that new computers do not include Excel. It must be purchased and installed before running it on your computer. If you do not want (or cannot afford) to purchase Excel, you can use a limited version for free at the Microsoft Office website.

If Excel is installed on your computer but isn't in your Start menu, use the following steps to launch Excel manually.

- Open My Computer or File Explorer.
- Click or select the C: drive. If Microsoft Office is installed on a drive other than the C: drive, select that drive instead.
- Find and open the Program Files (x86) or Program Files folder.
- Open the Microsoft Office folder.
- In the Microsoft Office folder, open the root folder. Then open the OfficeXX folder, where XX is the version of Microsoft Office (e.g., Office16 for Microsoft Office 2016) installed on your computer.
- Find and double-click the file named EXCEL.EXE to start the Excel program.

How To Open Microsoft Excel?

Running Excel is not different from running any other Windows program. If you are running Windows with a GUI like (Windows XP, Vista, and 7) follow the following steps.

- Click on the start menu

- Point to all programs
- Point to Microsoft Excel
- Click on Microsoft Excel
- Alternatively, you can also open it from the start menu if it has been added there. You can also open it from the desktop shortcut if you have created one.

For this book, we will be working with Windows 8.1 and Microsoft Excel 2013. Follow the following steps to run Excel on Windows 8.1

- Click on the start menu
- Search for Excel N.B. even before you even type, all programs starting with what you have typed will be listed.
- Click on Microsoft Excel

How To Open Microsoft Excel Without Using A Mouse

- Press the Windows key.
- Type Excel and select the Microsoft Excel entry in the search results.
- If Excel does not open after selecting it in the search results, press Enter to launch it.

How Can Excel Be Formatted?

Each of the rows, columns, and cells can be modified in many ways, including the background color, number or date format, size, text font, layout, etc. In our example above, you can see that the first row (row 1) has a blue background, bold text, and each cell has its text centered.

Download An Example Of A Spreadsheet File

We created a Microsoft Excel spreadsheet that you can download and open in any spreadsheet program, including Microsoft Excel. This spreadsheet illustrates some of the capabilities of a spreadsheet, formulas, and functions, and allows you to experiment more with a spreadsheet.

Why Do People Use Excel?

There are many reasons people use Excel. For example, someone might use Excel and a spreadsheet to keep track of their expenses. See our spreadsheet definition for a complete list of reasons and examples of how people use a spreadsheet.

What Is Excel Used for?

Excel is typically used to organize data and perform financial analysis. It is used across all business functions and at companies from small to large. To the average person, Excel is a number-crunching program, used to track household expenses or calculate complex formulas for school homework. However, the use of excel is capable of so much more and can be an incredibly powerful tool for businesses. The main uses of Excel include:

1. Data Entry And Storage

At its most basic level, Excel is an excellent tool for both data entry and storage. An Excel file's size is only limited by your device's computing power and memory. Worksheets can contain at most 1,048,576 rows and 16,384 columns. So obviously Excel can store a lot of data.

Not only that, features such as Data Form make it easy for data to be inputted and viewed, where users can create customized data entry forms tailored for their specific business needs. This can be used to build and maintain customer mailing lists or employee work shift lists.

2. Collection And Verification Of Business Data

Businesses often employ multiple systems (i.e CRM, inventory) each with its database and logs. All of which can be exported into Excel for easy access.

The program can also be used to clean up data, by removing incomplete or duplicate entries; eliminating such data from the beginning is necessary as it can impact later analysis and reporting.

3. Administrative And Managerial Duties

One aspect of managerial duties is creating and outlining business processes. This aids in process optimization and is an effective tool for organizing procedures and scenarios. The use of excel offers tools that allow users to create flow charts, which can include text, pictures, and animations.

4. Accounting And Budgeting

Excel even includes accounting and budgeting templates for easy use. From there the software's built-in calculating and formula features are available to help you organize and synthesize results.

5. Data Analysis

So you've been dumped with a giant pile of data and charged with drawing insights from it. Not to worry as Excel can also help you manage and synthesize clear communicable results from it.

One of the best features to do this is called Pivot Tables. They allow users to consolidate and focus on certain segments of data from a large data set, creating concise snapshots that can be used as an interactive summary report. By applying filters or swapping out data segments, the table can be effortlessly changed to display desired data fields.

6. Reporting + Visualizations

Data from both raw data sets and Pivot tables can even be used to create charts and graphs. Which can be used for formal reports, presentations, or aid in one's data analysis. As they can provide another perspective on trends and performance.

Excel again offers a variety of ready-made chart templates but also allows users to fine-tune details such as colors, axis values, and text comments. Visual reporting can be used in all sectors of business. For instance, marketing teams can use a column chart to report the efficacy of an ad campaign over time and compare it to previous campaigns.

7. Forecasting

While reporting and reviewing results is an important aspect of any business, forecasting and being prepared for various scenarios and changes is just as vital. The use of excel in conjunction with third-party software can be used when simulating financial projections by using past data. Excel can also use a chart's data set to create a formula that can be used to calculate future values.

The Excel Worksheet (Spreadsheet) And Workbook

An Excel worksheet, or spreadsheet, is a two-dimensional grid with columns and rows. Look at the worksheet below. The column names are letters of the alphabet starting with A, and rows are numbered chronologically starting with one. Each cell has an address or a cell reference: cells in Row #1 are A1, B1, C1, and so on. And cells in the first column are A1, A2, A3, etc.

Cell references are often used in math formulas or functions. For example, the formula to add the contents of cells B2 and B3 is: =B2+B3.

The Name Box is located in the area above Column A and displays the cell reference of the selected cell - the cell where the cursor is resting. In our spreadsheet above, the selected cell is A1. Notice that the column letter (A) and the row number (1) change color.

The beginning of the Formula Bar can be seen in the area above Column D on our worksheet. The Formula Bar displays the contents of the selected cell which may be a number, text, or formula. A workbook is a collection of worksheets. New workbooks, when created, contain three worksheets by default. Worksheet names are displayed on tabs at the bottom of the workbook.

How To Move From Cell To Cell

The arrow keys can be used to move left, right, up, and down from the current cell. Press the Enter key to move to the cell immediately below the current cell and press the Tab key to move one cell to the right.

How To Select Cells

There are a variety of ways to select cells in an Excel spreadsheet:

- To select one cell, click in the cell.
- To select one or more rows of cells, click on the row number(s).
- To select one or more columns of cells, click on the column letter(s).
- To select a group of contiguous cells, click in one corner cell and drag the mouse to the opposite corner. In the image at right, we have selected cells A1 through B5 (written A2:B5 in formulas).
- To select multiple cells that are not contiguous, press and hold the Ctrl key while clicking in the desired cells.
- To select every cell in the worksheet, click in the upper right corner of the worksheet to the left of "A."

How To Enter Data Into Cells

- To enter data into a cell, click in the cell and begin typing. What you type is also displayed in the Formula Bar. When entering dates, Excel defaults to the current year if the year portion of the date is omitted.

- Cell contents may be edited from the Formula Bar or directly inside a cell. To edit from the Formula Bar, select the cell and click inside the Formula Bar. When done typing, either press the Enter key or click inside another cell. To edit directly inside a cell, either double click inside the cell, or select the cell and press the F2 key.

- Each cell has a specific format that tells Excel how to display its contents. A cell's format may be different than the cell contents.

For example, if you enter 8.9521 in a cell formatted to show two decimal places, Excel will display 8.95 in the worksheet cell. However, Excel will use the actual value you entered when performing calculations that involve that cell.

How To Propagate Cell Contents

There are multiple ways to propagate or fill data from one cell to adjacent cells. Let's begin with two popular keyboard shortcuts that allow us to fill down, or fill to the right:

- To fill adjacent cells with the contents of the cell above, select the cell with the data and the cells to be filled and press Ctrl + D (the Ctrl key and the D key) to fill down.

- To fill adjacent cells with the contents of the cell to the left, select the cell with the data and cells to be filled and press Ctrl + R (the Ctrl key and the R key) to fill to the right.

- To propagate in any direction, use the Fill Handle to autofill. Click in a cell with data to be copied, hover the cursor over the cell's lower right corner until the cursor changes to a thin plus sign (+) or a dark square, and drag in any direction.

How To Move And Copy Cell Contents

- To move cell contents, right-click in the selected cell and click Cut; then right-click in the new location and click Paste. Similarly, to copy cell contents, right-click in the selected cell and select Copy, and paste in the new cell.

- To copy the contents of a cell range, click in one corner of the range, hold down the left mouse button, and drag to the opposite corner. Then highlight the same size cell range in the new location and Paste.

- Alternately, depending on the worksheet design, after copying you may be able to click in a cell and select "Insert Copied Cells" from the right-click menu.
- To remove the animated border around the original cell, press the ESC key, or start typing in a new cell.

How To Add And Delete Rows And Columns

- To insert a new row in a spreadsheet, right-click on a row number, and click Insert. Excel always inserts the row ABOVE the row that was clicked on. Press F4 to continue inserting additional rows.
- To delete a row, right-click on the row number, and click Delete. Contiguous rows can be deleted by highlighting them before clicking Delete. And non-contiguous rows can be selected by pressing and holding the CTRL key before clicking Delete. Don't press the Delete key on the keyboard—it will only delete the row's data.
- To insert a new column, right-click on a column letter and click Insert. Excel always inserts the column to the LEFT of the column that was clicked on. Press the F4 key to continue inserting additional columns.
- To delete a column, right-click on the column letter, and click Delete. Contiguous columns can be deleted by highlighting them before clicking Delete. And non-contiguous columns can be selected by pressing and holding the CTRL-key. Don't press the Delete key on the keyboard as it will only delete the column's data, not the actual column.

How To Lock Cells And Protect A Spreadsheet

There are two steps to preventing important cell content from being accidentally overwritten or deleted:

1. The cell must be locked, and
2. The worksheet must be protected.

If you have valuable data or complex formulas you cannot afford to lose, learn how to lock cells and protect worksheets.

Understanding The Ribbon

The ribbon provides shortcuts to commands in Excel. A command is an action that the user performs. An example of a command is creating a new document, printing a documenting, etc. The image below shows the ribbon used in Excel 2021.

Ribbon Components Explained

- **Ribbon Start Button:** It is used to access commands i.e. creating new documents, saving existing work, printing, accessing the options for customizing Excel, etc.
- **Ribbon Tabs:** The tabs are used to group similar commands together. The home tab is used for basic commands such as formatting the data to make it more presentable, sorting, and finding specific data within the spreadsheet.
- **Ribbon Bar:** The bars are used to group similar commands together. As an example, the Alignment ribbon bar is used to group all the commands that are used to align data together.

Understanding The Worksheet (Rows And Columns, Sheets, Workbooks)

A worksheet is a collection of rows and columns. When a row and a column meet, they form a cell. Cells are used to record data. Each cell is uniquely identified using a cell address. Columns are usually labeled with letters while rows are usually numbers.

A workbook is a collection of worksheets. By default, a workbook has three cells in Excel. You can delete or add more sheets to suit your requirements. By default, the sheets are named Sheet1, Sheet2, and so on. You can rename the sheet names to more meaningful names i.e. Daily Expenses, Monthly Budget, etc.

Customization Microsoft Excel Environment

I like the black colour, so my excel theme looks blackish. Your favorite color could be blue, and you too can make your theme color look blue-like. If you are not a programmer, you may not want to include ribbon tabs i.e. developer. All this is made possible via customizations. In this sub-section, we are going to look at;

- Customization the ribbon
- Setting the color theme
- Settings for formulas
- Proofing settings
- Save settings
- Customization of ribbon

The above image shows the default ribbon in Excel 2019. Let's start with customization of the ribbon, suppose you do not wish to see some of the tabs on the ribbon, or you would like to add some tabs that are missing such as the developer tab. You can use the options window to achieve this.

- Click on the ribbon start button
- Select options from the drop-down menu. You should be able to see an Excel Options dialog window
- Select the customize ribbon option from the left-hand side panel as shown below
- On your right-hand side, remove the checkmarks from the tabs that you do not wish to see on the ribbon. For this example, we have removed the Page Layout, Review, and View tab.
- Click on the "OK" button when you are done.
- Your ribbon will look as follows
- Adding custom tabs to the ribbon

You can also add your tab, give it a custom name and assign commands to it. Let's add a tab to the ribbon with the text MyCustomTab.

- Right-click on the ribbon and select Customize the Ribbon. The dialogue window shown above will appear
- Click on the new tab button
- Select the newly created tab
- Click on Rename button
- Give it the name of MyCustomTab
- Select the New Group (Custom) under the MyCustomTab tab as shown in the image below
- Click on Rename button and give it the name of My Commands
- Let's now add commands to my ribbon bar

- The commands are listed on the middle panel
- Select the All chart types command and click on Add button
- Click on OK

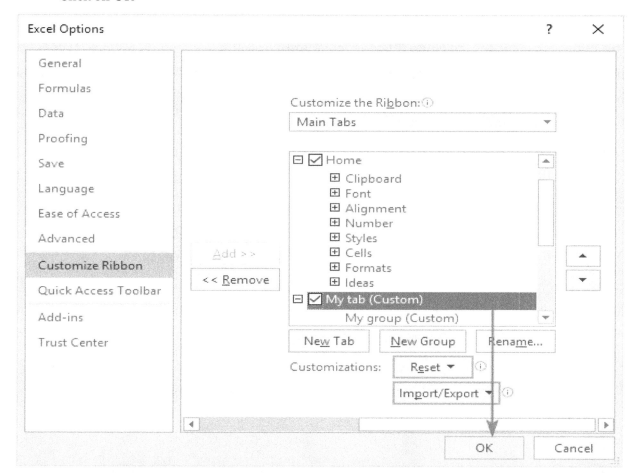

Setting The Color Theme

To set the color theme for your Excel sheet you have to go to the Excel ribbon and click on the File Option command. It will open a window where you have to follow the following steps.

- The general tab on the left-hand panel will be selected by default.
- Look for the color scheme under General options for working with Excel
- Click on the color scheme drop-down list and select the desired color
- Click on the OK button

Settings For Formulas

This option allows you to define how Excel behaves when you are working with formulas. You can use it to set options i.e. autocomplete when entering formulas, change the cell referencing style, and use numbers for both columns and rows and other options. If you want to activate an option, click on its check box. If you want to deactivate an option, remove the mark from the checkbox. You can this option from the Options dialogue window under the formulas tab from the left-hand side panel

Proofing settings

This option manipulates the entered text entered into excel. It allows setting options such as the dictionary language that should be used when checking for wrong spellings, suggestions from the dictionary, etc. You can this option from the options dialogue window under the proofing tab from the left-hand side panel

Save Settings

This option allows you to define the default file format when saving files, enable auto-recovery in case your computer goes off before you could save your work, etc. You can use this option from the Options dialogue window under the save tab from the left-hand side panel.

Why Would Someone Use Excel Over Another Spreadsheet Program?

Today, there are many free spreadsheet programs that someone could use instead of Excel. However, even with the available free options, Excel remains the most-used spreadsheet because of all its available options, features, and because many businesses still use the program.

Tip

- Even with all Excel's options, a free spreadsheet program like Google Sheets is often all most users need.

Note

- If you want to get Excel because it's a job requirement, it's still okay to learn all the basics in a free spreadsheet program. However, there are still many differences between Excel and a free spreadsheet program.

Importance of Ms Excel In Our Daily And Business Lives:

1. Easy Arithmetic Solutions

Perhaps the most important use of MS Excel is using its ability of mass arithmetic calculations. With a vast program full of formulae, it can add, subtract, multiply and divide hundreds of numbers altogether, and can easily re-do it if a value is changed or added. This feature can be used to easily make a company's yearly sales and other spreadsheets.

2. Formatting Options

The various formatting options, including italics, highlighting, and colors, allow businesses to bring the most important data to be different from the rest. Several tasks achieved through this tool are beyond impressive, with an entire row highlighting and comparing lists and values to name a few. You can use them to highlight specific entries in Accounting.

3. Availability Of Online Access

Excel is part of the Office 365 Productivity Suite, Which means that business employers and their employees can easily access their files over the cloud network, free from the bondage of file transfer. Using a web-enabled PC, mobile, or tablet, you can use the same program and access the same file remotely, making it easy to do changes if you can't access your PC and need to send the spreadsheet immediately!

4. Charts For Analysis

If you are working in a large association where the boss wants a detailed visual representation of the various sectors of the business, you'll need to draw charts. MS Excel makes it easy to do so! After filtering and correctly inputting data, you can turn it into a Pie Chart or Clustered Columns with a single click. Even better, it allows you to customize the colors and boundaries of the charts and pie diagrams!

5. Bring All The Data In One Place

Containing over 1,048,576 rows and 16,384 columns each in the spreadsheet, with hundreds of them, or even more, if your PC is capable, in a single file, Excel allows you to create spreadsheets bigger than 20 A1 papers! You can import data from other spreadsheets and add pictures and other objects through the insert tab, making it easy to put all the data you collected in various files in one place.

6. Human Resource Planning

Although there are other systems such as Oracle, or QuickBooks for planning this, Excel allows you to manage it all in one file! You can summarise an employee's expenses, their pay per hour, and easily discover wrong entries. Human Resource Professionals use this to take the whole employee journal in bulk and use it to plan future credit and decide whether to invest more or not, making it important for the control of the future.

What Are The Different Versions Of Microsoft Excel?

Microsoft Excel has had many versions throughout its history. The different releases with their release dates are listed below.

Windows Versions

- Excel 2021, released in 2021
- Excel 2019, released in 2018
- Office 365 and Excel 2016, released in 2016
- Excel 2013, released in 2013
- Excel 2010, released in 2010
- Excel 2007, released in 2007
- Excel 2003, released in 2003
- Excel 2002, released in 2002
- Excel 2000, released in 2000
- Excel 97, released in 1997
- Excel 95, released in 1995
- Excel 5.0, released in 1993
- Excel 4.0, released in 1992
- Excel 3.0, released in 1990
- Excel 2.0, released in 1987

Mac versions

- Excel 2019, released in 2018
- Excel 2016, released in 2016
- Excel 2011, released in 2011
- Excel 2008, released in 2008
- Excel 2004, released in 2004
- Excel 2001, released in 2001
- Excel 2000, released in 2000
- Excel 98, released in 1998
- Excel 5.0, released in 1993
- Excel 4.0, released in 1992
- Excel 3.0, released in 1990

- Excel 2.2, released in 1989
- Excel 1.5, released in 1988
- Excel 1, released in 1985

What Came Before Excel?

Microsoft Excel was not the first spreadsheet program. Lotus 1-2-3 and VisiCalc were popular spreadsheet programs released before Excel.

MS Excel – Points To Remember

There are certain things which one must know concerning MS Excel, its applications, and usage:

- An MS Excel file is saved with an extension of .xls
- Companies with large staff and workers use MS Excel as saving employee information becomes easier
- Excel spreadsheets are also used in hospitals where the information of patients can be saved more easily and can be removed conveniently once their medical history is cleared
- The sheet on which you work is called a Worksheet
- Multiple worksheets can be added in a single Excel file
- This is a data processing application

Best Practices When Working With Microsoft Excel

- Save workbooks with backward compatibility in mind. If you are not using the latest features in higher versions of Excel, you should save your files in 2003 *.xls format for backward compatibility
- Use descriptive names for columns and worksheets in a workbook
- Avoid working with complex formulas with many variables. Try to break them down into small managed results that you can use to build on
- Use built-in functions whenever you can instead of writing your formulas

CHAPTER 2: FEATURES OF MICROSOFT EXCEL

Features Of Excel

Features of Excel made the Excel most widely used application. Excel is a very popular application because of its wide range of features and powerful tools. Microsoft added many features in each release of Excel 2007, 2010, 2013, 2016, and Office Online 365. Here are the main features of Microsoft Excel.

Main Features Of Excel

We can divide the Main features of the Excel into Graphical, Data Base and Functional Features:

1. Graphical Features Of Excel

Excel has a variety of graphical features to represent the data in Charts and pictorial format.

- **Charts:** We can use charts to represent the data in rich visualized graphical representation.
- **Shapes:** We can create a variety of shapes to represent the data in shapes and info graphics. We can draw any shape with the free form feature in Excel.
- **SmartArt:** We can use SmartArt to align the data in creative designs and visually communicate the information.
- **Clip Arts:** We can add ready-to-use clip arts to convey our message in pictorial representation.
- **Pictures:** We can insert any image to enhance the objects. Example backgrounds of Worksheets, Shapes, and Charts.

2. DataBase Features of Excel

Excel can be used as a database and perform a variety of data operations.

- **PivotTables:** We can use the Summarize the data and create powerful cross tables.
- **Slicers:** Slicers are introduced in Excel 2010, this will help us to connect the multiple pivot tables and filter the data with buttons.
- **Tables:** We can create the tables in the data in records and fields format. This will be helpful to quickly perform further analysis.
- **Sparklines:** Introduced in Excel 2010, we can insert the lightweight charts into the cells.

- **Database:** We can use Excel as a Database to store the 1 million records. We can connect to a variety of databases and import the data into Excel.
- **Sorting:** We can sort the data in Excel. We can sort Ascending or Descending with one or more columns.
- **Filtering:** We can Filter the data in Excel. We can set a variety of options to filter with the required options. Excel has the Advanced Filtering option to perform the more complex filters.
- **Data Validations:** Data Validation Feature helps to restrict the cell to accept a certain type of data. We can also provide the drop-down to choose from the pre-defined list.
- **Grouping:** We can group the rows and columns with parent and child records.

3. Functional Features Of Excel

Excel Tools and Functions will help to perform powerful calculations and enhance the Excel Application Features.

- **Functions:** There are more than 300 built-in formulas to use in the Excel Cells. Verity of the formulas (Text, Date, String, Maths, etc) will help to perform a variety of calculations.
- **VBA Macros:** Excel comes with VBA Programming. We can use the Macros feature to automate repetitive tasks.
- **Add-ins:** We can develop the Excel Add-ins with VBA or .NET to enhance the Excel Functionality.
- **Hyperlinks:** We can add hyperlinks in Excel to quickly navigate the different parts of the Excel Workbook.
- **Conditional Format:** We can format the data based on certain conditions. This helps to highlight the significant data range.
- **SpellCheck:** Built-in spell check feature helps us to avoid spelling and grammatical errors in the data.
- **Protection:** Excel provides Workbook, Worksheet, and VBA Protection options.

Excel Provides, variety of Add-ins for Data analysis and ETL process. We can use Excel for a wide range of applications. Here are the uses of MS Excel. Excel has introduced a ribbon menu in Office 2007 and added a variety of features in each release:

1. Features Of Excel 2007

The main new feature in Excel 2007 is Excel Ribbon Menu. And many more useful features:

- **Ribbon Menu:** Excel introduced a ribbon menu in 2007, the look and feel of Excel is more modern
- **Open XML:** Introduced Open XML File structure
- **More Rows And Columns:** This addition allows to store more records and fields in each spreadsheet
- **Themes And Styles:** This feature helps to easily switch from one color schema to another
- Improvements and added features in Formulas, Charts, and PivotTables

2. Features Of Excel 2010

The main New features in Excel 2010 is Slicers and Sparklines:

- **Slicers:** Excel Slicers for PivotTable helps to filter the multiple PivotTable with one button Click
- **Sparklines:** Now you can create dashboards with graphs in Cells with the Sparkline feature
- Mobile Excel for Windows 7 and many more Performance Features added in Excel 2010

3. Features Of Excel 2013

Excel was MDI(Multiple Document Interface) till Excel 2010, now it is a Single Document Application. Smart and Modern look and feel of the Application, and much more performance features introduced in Excel 2013.

- New Start Screen is introduced in Excel 2013
- The ribbon menu is enhanced, now it's similar to Windows 8/10 application menu
- Quick tools for Charts
- Quick Data Analysis Tools introduced in Excel 2013
- Enhanced Graphics and Picture Quality in Excel 2013.
- Added many more color schema XML files.

4. Features Of Excel 2016

Excel 2016 is almost looking like Excel 2013.

Tell me what you want to do?: New tool to quickly search commands

- **New Charts:** Sunburst, Waterfall, Histograms, and Pareto charts
- **Scalable Vector Graphics:** Now we can insert SVGs in Excel
- **Icons:** New command to browse the office icons and insert the ready to use vector icons
- The pen is added to draw the shapes

5. Features of Excel 2021

New tool to quickly search commands

- **Data visualization with Insights.** Enter Insights, a new feature on the Ribbon that will make lots of suggestions of great visual ways to see your data. Some you may have thought of, some will probably be new ideas.

- **Funnel and 2D map charts.** A funnel chart is a type of chart commonly used to illustrate the states in a process. For example, if you wanted to see the amount of closed sales versus the total amount of leads that were followed, you could use a funnel chart to visualize this. To use Insights, make sure you've at least clicked on a cell in an existing range of data, and then select Insert à Insights.

- **Geografic and stock Data** We can now stop wasting precious time using Google searches on readily available data and let Excel pull in the information for us. Right now, this functionality exists for stock and geographic data, but there's no reason to doubt that won't increase to more data lookups in the future.

Uses of Microsoft Excel In Business

What are the uses of Microsoft Excel in the workplace? The list of ways that business uses MS Excel is long. But we've broken it down to a top 10 list.

At a basic level, MS Excel is used for storing information, analyzing and sorting, and reporting. It's extremely popular in business because spreadsheets are highly visual and fairly easy to use.

Some of the most common business uses of MS Excel are for business analysis, managing human resources, performance reporting, and operations management. We know this for a fact after analyzing job data (using MS Excel).

1. Business Analysis

The number 1 use of MS Excel in the workplace is to do business analysis.

Business analysis is essentially using collected data to inform decision-making. Businesses naturally gather data in their day-to-day activities, which may be data on product sales, website traffic, spending on supplies, insurance claims, etc.

Business analysis is the activity of converting data into something useful to the people who run the business. For example, you could run a profitability report by the day of the week. If the business always loses money on a Sunday, then that's information management could use to make a decision (such as closing on Sundays).

Job Examples: Business analyst, business planning analyst, business solutions analyst, claims analyst, collections analyst, credit officer, data analyst, data and audience analyst, finance business analyst, investment operations portfolio analyst, junior data analyst, regional finance analyst, senior data analyst, senior finance analyst, senior portfolio analyst.

2. People Management

You may be surprised to learn that one of the top uses of Excel in business is to manage people. MS Excel is a powerful way to organize information about people, whether they are employees, customers, supporters, or training attendees.

Using Excel, personal information can be stored and retrieved efficiently. A spreadsheet row or column can be used for an individual record that may include information like name, email address, employee start date, items purchased, subscription status, and last contact.

Job Examples: Client growth coordinator, client management and administration, client relationship manager, client service manager, client service specialist, employer service consultant, HR administrator, human resources administrative assistant, human resources administrator, human resources adviser, human resources officer, junior HR analyst, reconciliation and payments officer, relationship manager.

3. Managing Operations

Excel is relied on heavily to manage the day-to-day operations of many businesses. Business activities can often involve quite complicated logistics. Inventory flows need to be controlled so that you can keep operations running smoothly and without overstocking on particular items. That means keeping track of supplier and client transactions, listing critical dates, and managing times and schedules.

While Amazon uses sophisticated custom software for operations management, MS Excel is an important tool for many smaller businesses (or parts of larger businesses). An advantage of Excel is that it's relatively low-tech, allowing it to be used by many people and without the risk of programming bugs.

Job Examples: Business operations analyst, data operations manager, graduate program – supply chain and operations, in market supply chain analyst, operational business analyst, operational enablement associate, operational knowledge management specialist, supply chain associate, supply chain specialist.

4. Performance Reporting

Performance monitoring and reporting is a specialized type of business analysis that can be done effectively using MS Excel. For example, many accountants still use Excel (partly because it's compatible with cloud-based accounting software).

A common way to convert data into a performance report in Excel is to create a pivot table. By inserting a pivot table and linking it to data, you can extra useful information from the dataset quickly. Pivot tables have numerous in-built functions that allow for tasks such as counting and summing certain types of data within the dataset.

Job Examples: Financial accountant, forecast analyst/sales support, performance analyst, performance analyst – procurement, professional services operations analyst, reporting analyst, reporting development analyst, sales coordinator, sales operations analyst.

5. Office Administration

Underlining the importance of Microsoft Excel, office administrators use Excel to enter and store key administrative data. The same data may be subsequently used for accounting and financial reporting, as well as business analysis and performance reporting.

Apart from recordkeeping, Excel is useful in office administration for supporting day-to-day tasks such as invoicing, paying bills, and contacting suppliers and clients. It's an all-purpose tool for keeping track of and managing office activities.

Job Examples: Administration assistant, administration officer, administration supervisor, administrative assistant, business operations and office manager, junior clerical and administrative officer, office admin manager, office support maintenance/ general duties.

6. Strategic Analysis

Concerning the use of Excel, strategic analysis is where business decisions are closely connected to the data and formulas on spreadsheets. You apply Excel to guide actions such as investments and asset allocations.

As an example, based on an Excel model, you may decide to take out currency insurance. Spreadsheet analysis is designed to inform business decisions in a specific way.

Job Examples: Asset manager, realty management division, mergers and acquisitions valuations – analyst, membership and campaigns strategist, portfolio administration associate, portfolio analyst, portfolio associate – wealth management, portfolio management officer – asset finance.

7. Project Management

Although project managers have access to purpose-built project management (BPM) software, an Excel Workbook is often an effective alternative. Projects are business activities that typically have a budget and start and end dates. Project plans can be placed into a workbook, which can then be used to track progress and keep the project on schedule. An advantage of using Excel is that you can easily share the project workbook with others, including people who are unfamiliar with, or lack access to, custom PM software.

Job Examples: Project analyst, project assistant/officer (IT), project business analyst.

8. Managing Programs

Excel is a good platform for managing programs. It can be adapted to handle the specific characteristics of a given program. And, because MS Excel is widely known, program records can easily be managed by multiple people and, when the time comes, handed over to a new manager. A program is like a project, but it may be ongoing and can depend on participation by users. MS Excel helps managers allocate resources, keep track of progress, and maintain participant records.

Job Examples: Event coordinator, learning and development officer, learning and development coordinator, manager – internships, programs and office coordinator, records and results coordinator, training administrator.

9. Contract Administration

Contract administrators like to use MS Excel because it provides a no-fuss means of recording contract details, including dates, milestones, deliverables, and payments. Many different contract management templates are available, and these can be adapted to suit the particular contract type or stage of the contract lifecycle.

Job Examples: Building contract administrator, contracts administrator, estimator/contracts administrator, graduate contracts administrator, lease administrator, quote and tender administrator.

10. Account Management

Account managers are generally required to be competent MS Excel users since they receive and need to maintain customer records. The job of an account manager is to nurture relationships with existing clients of the business. Key goals are to achieve customer loyalty and repeat sales. It's a marketing kind of role and a popular career for MBA graduates. Excel is commonly used in account management since it provides a simple way to share and maintain client files.

Job Examples: Account coordinator, advertising manager, design studio account manager, digital account manager, junior account manager.

Why You Need Excel Skills In Business

If this list hasn't convinced you already, MS Excel skills are very useful in the workplace.

Not all jobs use Excel and those that do are often considered 'middle skill' jobs. However, Excel is widely used. Having good spreadsheet skills, therefore, gives you the ability to work on all sorts of different tasks. And you can more easily get value out of information that's being shared in workbooks.

Once you know how to use Excel, you'll find yourself using it more and more. It's an accessible platform that can be used to do both simple and highly sophisticated business tasks.

CHAPTER 3 : MICROSOFT EXCEL PROBLEM AND SOLUTION

Excel Spreadsheet Problems And How To Solve Them

If you need to make a list of anything, it's tempting to see Excel as the default repository: after all, it's only a small list of items for yourself or a few close colleagues.

7 Excel Spreadsheet Problems And How To Solve Them

Perhaps you need something more sophisticated, such as formulas for calculations or macro programming to automate data collection and processing.

Unfortunately, the ease with which you can start working in Excel or a rival spreadsheet program is also one of its biggest problems. What begins as a small project in Excel grows into something massive, at which point you could also face speed and stability issues or even a development problem you can't solve.

Furthermore, big data management tasks often present significant challenges, such as organization, implementation, classification of files, database management, user collaboration, and more. All it takes to break the structure of a database is placing data in the wrong area, typing data inconsistently, or even having two people working on the same sheet. Several things can go wrong, causing time delays and possible data loss.

This e-book explains the most common issues that come up when using Excel spreadsheets, how to tackle them, and when you're better off taking the plunge and switching to a database instead.

Issue 1: Excel Multi-User Editing

When Excel systems grow organically, you quickly run into problems where one user opens a workbook at any particular time, and a second person gets told that it's already open. The second user can cancel, wait, or view a read-only version. Excel's promise to let you know when the other person exits the workbook is a gamble since it doesn't check the status that often, and it may never enlighten you. Even if it does, someone else might log in and open the file before you.

- Open your desired Spreadsheet and click on File at the top. Excel File tab
- Next, in the menu on the left-hand side, click on Share to open up a new window. Excel File
- Now, enter the information of the user you want to share the Spreadsheet with. Excel Share
- You can also split the data into several workbooks so that different people work on different workbooks without treading on each other's toes.

Issue 2: Excel Shared Workbooks

Excel Online allows multiple editors, by default, but it's missing a great deal of functionality. The service isn't much of a contender for anything but the simplest tasks. Although the Shared Workbooks feature looks like it should do the job, it's full of restrictions. You can't create a table or delete a block of cells if the workbook is shared, for example.

When Excel systems grow organically, you run into the problem that only one user can open a workbook at any one time. There are workarounds for some online Excel restrictions. For others, it's a matter of changing the workbook's structure rather than using a workbook already set up but this scenario often gets in the way. As a result, it is impossible to use a shared workbook in the same way you might use an ordinary, single-user workbook.

Changes in shared workbooks are synchronized between users each time the workbook gets saved. This action gets placed on a timed schedule, forcing a save every five minutes, for example. However, the overhead of regular saving and the tracking of every user's changes is quite large. Workbooks can quickly balloon in size and put a strain on your network, slowing down other systems.

Issue 3: Excel Linked Workbooks

Splitting your data across multiple workbooks can provide a workaround to the problem of multi-user editing. Still, they will likely need to have links between them so that values entered in one get used in another. Links between workbooks are also useful for keeping separate data in separate files, rather than having individual sheets in one workbook.

Annoyingly, these links are another source of frustration and instability. They become absolute, including the full path to the source workbook, or relative, including the difference between the source and destination paths. Although this sounds sensible, Excel employs arcane rules to decide when to use each type of link and change them.

The rules are governed by several options and by whether the workbooks got saved before inserting links. The links also change when you save the workbook or open and use Save As to make a duplicate, rather than copy the file using File Explorer. The upshot of all this confusion and uncertainty is that the links between workbooks break easily, and recovering from broken links is a time-consuming process. Nobody gets access to the files affected.

Linked data is only updated when the files get opened unless you specifically click Data > Queries & Connections > Edit Links > Update Values. Here's a quick demonstration.

Open up your desired Spreadsheet and click on Data at the top. Excel Menu

Now, locate Queries & Connections and click on Edit Links. Excel settings

Then, select Update Values.

If your links aren't between two workbooks but cover three or more, you have to open all the workbooks in the correct order to ensure any updated data processes are in the right order, from the first to the second to the third. If you changed a value in the first workbook and then opened the third, it wouldn't see any changes because the second workbook hadn't updated its values.

This data chaining is logical, but it increases the likelihood that information is either incorrect or that you'll try to open a workbook that someone else is already editing.

Of course, you can try to avoid linked workbooks altogether, but there's a chance you'll end up entering the same data into more than one workbook, and with that comes the danger of typing it in slightly differently each time.

Issue 4: Excel Data Validation

Errors can creep into data within any computer system: people mistype words or transpose digits in numbers with monotonous regularity. If your data doesn't get checked as it's entered, you're going to have problems.

By default, Excel accepts whatever the user types. It is possible to set up validation on look-up lists, but these are difficult to maintain, mainly if the same field gets used in more than one place. If users have to enter document ID numbers or customer reference numbers without any checks, it's easy to tie the wrong records together without realizing it. The data integrity of the system becomes fatally compromised, and any analysis of the data is suspect.

You may already suffer the effects of data validation problems without realizing the root cause. Consider a situation where you have a list of invoices in Excel. The user types the name of the customer slightly differently on each invoice. As a result, you get invoices to "Jones Ltd," "Jones Limited," "Jones Ltd," and "jones." You may be aware that these are all referring to the same company, but Excel doesn't. Any analysis of the invoice data, such as a pivot table based on customers by month, delivers multiple results when there should only be one.

Issue 5: Excel Navigation

Large workbooks are challenging to navigate. The sheet tabs across the bottom of the window are a terrible mechanism for finding your way around when there are numerous amounts of them. With more displayable tabs across the screen, it becomes difficult to find what you need. Here's a quick way to navigate through sheets.

Near the bottom, on the left side of the screen, right-click on the arrows buttons, to the left of the sheet names, to bring up the Activate Sheet dialog. Excel Activate Sheet button

Only the first 20 sheets are listed before you have to scroll through the list. There's no way to sort, group, or search for the sheet you want. The window should look something like the one shown below. Excel Activate Window

Issue 6: Excel Security

You can add security to Excel workbooks, but it's rife with problems. Protection is geared much more towards protecting the structure of the workbook rather than the data. You can try to lock some sheets and cells to stop users from changing the structure and formula, but if they can see the data, they can usually change any or all of it (unless you do some creative macro programming).

Issue 7: Excel Speed Problems

Excel isn't the fastest application, and its programming language, VBA, is sluggish compared to more professional programming languages such as C#. This scenario stems from the intended use and flexible nature of Excel. It is, after all, a spreadsheet engine. Yes, Excel VBA can be pressed into service to manage lists of data, but that doesn't mean it's the best choice for that kind of work. Other applications are better suited to such tasks—mainly because they get explicitly designed to do them.

Common Excel Problems That Can Be Solved Quickly

Are you having an assignment due tomorrow and can't get over MS-excel recurring issues? It's obvious, Microsoft excel users find themselves encountering few problems throughout the process. No denying! Microsoft struggles can drive you mad! It can be frustrating as hell, given the time it takes to fix these issues.

To Back You Up, We Have Listed Five Standard Excel Repair Solutions.

1. Excel Not Responding: The time when your excel freezes or stops working is a time of real stress. It is obvious to worry that excel will force the program to close, and all your workings will be gone just like that! It's a common problem reported by many excel users. The hanging or freezing of excel can be due to:

- Outdated antivirus software.
- When you haven't installed the latest update.

- Prior installed add-in interferes with excel.
- Advance troubleshooting.
- Excel is in use by a different process.

Solution 1: To fix the freezing of excel, you are suggested to install the latest update. Installing recommended updates often fixes any loopholes or other vulnerabilities and also replaces outdated files. So update!

2. Added formulas performance issue: The slow performance issue can drive you nuts. The formulas that impact an entire column can invite performance issues in excel formats like XLSX. This problem is often faced because of the grown column size in updated excel software like MS excel 2010.

Solution 2: To resolve the issue, excel users are recommended to adjust the slow calculating worksheet to perform hundreds or even thousands of times faster. To boost the speed, all you need to do is set the calculation mode from automatic to manual calculation. And then you are good to go!

3. All Hashes In The Cell: Is your cell filled with hashes? Well, that can be due to reasons owing to:

- When the value of the cell doesn't fit in the cell's width.
- When the text or number exceeds 253 characters.
- Date and time written in negative format. (It should always be positive)

Solution 3:
- To repair excel having this issue try-
- Increasing the column width using shortcut ALT OCA or ALT OCW
- Cut off the number of characters or shorten the cell value.
- Assure data is not in a negative format.

Formulas Not Working: Sometimes, when you enter a formula, you get the formula itself displayed in the cell instead of the result. This problem is because the cell has text format, which Excel interprets as a piece of text.

Solution: To overcome this, try converting the cell in general or number format and then enter the formula once again. I hope this works!

4. Corrupted Workbook File: Microsoft excel launches the recovery mode by default when the workbook is corrupted. However, if users still can't open it, they need to repair the workbook manually. To do this, follow the following steps-

Solution 4:

- Select the Ms-office button, then open the dialogue box
- Then select the corrupted file and choose "open and repair" to repair and restore as much data as possible.
- In case the repair is not successful, select "extract data."

5. Users can then revert to the last version of the workbook file available. Users can also try saving the file in SYLK format to cut off any corrupted data or details (Save as > SYLK)

Solution 5: Though the problems occurring in excel are not just limited to five. This write-up has covered the most common excel repairs that occur often. I hope this saved you from scratching your head and being frustrated with excel issues.

How To Learn Excel: 5 Tips From Microsoft Training Experts

Most business professionals have dabbled in Microsoft Excel, but few ever master the platform. Excel is a sophisticated software with loads of functionality beneath its surface, and it can seem intimidating to learn.

However, Excel is not as challenging to learn as many people believe. With the right training and practice, you can improve your Excel skills and open yourself up to more job opportunities. 80 percent of middle-skills jobs require spreadsheet and word processing abilities.

5 Tips For Learning Excel

When you look at all the things Excel can do, you might get overwhelmed. There's so much to cover, and it never seems like there's enough time. Instead of trying to go over everything at once, take a step back. The best way to learn Excel is to break it down into bite-size components. Here's how:

1. Practice Simple Math Problems In Excel

When it comes to Excel, it's easiest to start with basic math. That way, you can get a handle on typing into Excel and get comfortable with its abilities before jumping into more complex tasks, such as learning functions and types of formatting.

The main thing you need to know is that Excel wants to see an equals sign first. In other words, when you're writing "1 plus 1," you need to type "=1+1" into the cell. After you press "enter," the cell will display the number "2." You can do the same thing with subtraction, multiplication (using an asterisk "*"), and division (using a forward slash "/").

2. Learn How To Create Tables

While using Excel to perform basic math is helpful, it's probably not the primary reason you need to learn the software. Most likely, you need to organize data, and creating tables is a great way to start.

To begin, select the data set all of it, including headings, you want to convert into a table. Then, choose the "Quick Analysis" option that pops up at the bottom corner of your selection. From there, you can select "Table" from the "Tables" tab in Excel.

Your data will immediately change, and you'll be able to manipulate it in different ways. For example, you'll be able to filter out specific data or sort information in different ways.

3. Learn How To Create Charts

Now that you know how to create a table, it's time to learn how to create graphs or charts. The steps are similar to creating a table, but you need to decide which type of chart or graph you'll want ahead of time. Excel can give you some suggestions on how to visualize your graph, but the decision is ultimately up to you. Once you know which chart or graph you want, follow the same steps for creating a table above, but go to "Charts" instead of "Tables." You'll be able to hover over each option to see how the visual will look, and you can select "More" for additional options and control over the final product.

4. Take Excel Training Courses

When it comes to learning just about anything, taking a training course or two can't hurt. The more advanced you become, the less you'll need to update spreadsheets manually, and the more time you'll have to focus on your important tasks. The right training courses can help you master everything from formulas and charts to pivot tables and conditional formatting. They can even help you further understand the data you're putting into Excel and analyze it for better insights.

5. Earn A Microsoft Office Specialist Certification

Once you've become an advanced Microsoft Excel user, a certification program will help you demonstrate to current and potential employers that you truly understand the software. And what could be better than getting certified by Microsoft itself?

Excel Not Responding, Hangs, Freezes, Or Stops Working

This article discusses troubleshooting steps that can help resolve the most common issues when you receive an Excel not responding error, Excel hangs or freezes when you launch it or open an Excel workbook. These types of problems may occur for one or more of the reasons listed below.

Follow the provided solutions in this article in order. If you have previously tried one of these methods, and it did not help, please go to the next solution on the list.

Start Excel In Safe Mode

Safe mode lets you start Excel without encountering certain startup programs. You can open Excel in safe mode by pressing and holding Ctrl while you start the program, or by using the /safe switch (excel.exe /safe) when you start the program from the command line. When you run Excel in safe mode, it bypasses functionality and settings such as alternative startup location, changed toolbars, the xlstart folder, and Excel add-ins. However, COM add-ins are excluded.

- If your issue is resolved after you run Excel in safe mode, see: How to troubleshoot startup problems in Excel.
- If your issue is not resolved after you start Excel in safe mode, continue to the next item on this list.

Install The Latest Updates

You might need to set Windows Update to automatically download, and install recommended updates. Installing any important recommendation, and optimal updates can often correct problems by replacing out-of-date files and fixing vulnerabilities. To install the latest Office updates, follow the steps in this article: Update Office and your computer.

- If installing the latest Office updates did not resolve your issue, continue to the next item on this list.

Check To Make Sure Excel Is Not In Use By Another Process

If Excel is in use by another process, this information will be displayed in the status bar at the bottom of the Excel window. If you try to perform other actions while Excel is in use, Excel may not respond. Let the task in process finish its job before attempting other actions. If Excel is not is used by another process, continue to the next item on the list.

Investigate Possible Issues With Add-Ins

While add-ins can enhance your experience, they can occasionally interfere, or conflict with Excel. Try starting Excel without add-ins to see if the problem goes away.

Do One Of The Following:

- If you are running Windows 10, choose Start > All apps > Windows System > Run > type Excel /safe in the Run box, then click OK.

- If you are running Windows 8, click Run in the Apps menu > type Excel /safe in the Run box, then click OK.

- If you are running Windows 7, click Start > type Excel /safe in Search programs and files, then click OK.

- If the issue is resolved, click File > Options > Add-ins.

- Select COM Add-ins, and click Go.

- Clear all the checkboxes in the list, and click OK.

- Close and restart Excel.

If the issue does not occur when you restart Excel, start enabling your add-ins one at a time until does. This will allow you to figure out which add-in is causing the problem. Be sure and restart Excel each time you enable an add-in. If disabling add-ins did not resolve your issue, continue to the next item on the list.

Investigate Excel File Details And Contents

Excel files can exist on the computer for a long time. They are upgraded from version to version and frequently travel from one user to another user. Frequently, a user inherits an Excel file but doesn't know what is included in the file. The following things can cause performance or crashing issues:

- Formulas referencing entire columns.

- Array formulas referencing an uneven number of elements in the arguments.

- Hundreds, or perhaps thousands of hidden or 0 height and width objects.

- Excessive styles are caused by frequent copying and pasting between workbook.

- Excessive, and invalid defined names.

CHAPTER 4: MICROSOFT EXCEL FORMULAS

Microsoft Excel is the go-to tool for working with data. There are probably a handful of people who haven't used Excel, given its immense popularity. Excel is a widely used software application in industries today, built to generate reports and business insights. Excel supports several in-built applications that make it easier to use.

Excel Formulas

Excel formulas help you identify relationships between values in the cells of your spreadsheet, perform mathematical calculations using those values, and return the resulting value in the cell of your choice. Formulas you can automatically perform include sum, subtraction, percentage, division, average, and event dates/times.

One such feature that allows Excel to stand out is - Excel formulas. In this article, we'll be discussing the various Microsoft Excel functions and formulas. These formulas and functions enable you to perform calculations and data analysis faster. Here, we will look into the top 15 Excel formulas that one must know while working on Excel. The topics that we will be covering in this ebook are as follows:

- What is Excel Formula?
- Excel Formulas and Functions

What Is Excel Formula?

In Microsoft Excel, a formula is an expression that operates on values in a range of cells. These formulas return a result, even when it is an error. Excel formulas enable you to perform calculations such as addition, subtraction, multiplication, and division. In addition to these, you can find out averages and calculate percentages in excel for a range of cells, manipulate date and time values, and do a lot more.

There is another term that is very familiar to Excel formulas, and that is "function". The two words, "formulas" and "functions" are sometimes interchangeable. They are closely related, but yet different. A formula begins with an equal sign. Meanwhile, functions are used to perform complex calculations that cannot be done manually. Functions in excel have names that reflect their intended use.

The example below shows how we have used the multiplication formula manually with the '*' operator.

The example below shows how we have used the function - 'PRODUCT' to perform multiplication. As you can see, we didn't use the mathematical operator here.

Excel formulas and functions help you perform your tasks efficiently, and it's time-saving. Let's proceed and learn the different types of functions available in Excel and use relevant formulas as and when required.

Basic Terms In Excel

There are two basic ways to perform calculations in Excel: Formulas and Functions.

1. Formulas

In Excel, a formula is an expression that operates on values in a range of cells or a cell. For example, =A1+A2+A3, which finds the sum of the range of values from cell A1 to cell A3.

2. Functions

Functions are predefined formulas in Excel. They eliminate laborious manual entry of formulas while giving them human-friendly names. For example: =SUM(A1:A3). The function sums all the values from A1 to A3.

How To Enter A Formula

To Enter A Formula:

- Select a cell
- Enter an equals sign (=)
- Type the formula, and press enter.

Instead of typing cell references, you can point and click, as seen below. Note references are color-coded.

All formulas in Excel must begin with an equals sign (=). No equals sign, no formula:

- Forgot to enter an equals sign means no formula, just text

How To Change A Formula

To edit a formula, you have 3 options:

- Select the cell, edit in the formula bar

- Double-click the cell, edit directly
- Select the cell, press F2, edit directly

No matter which option you use, press Enter to confirm changes when done. If you want to cancel and leave the formula unchanged, click the Escape key.

Excel Formulas And Functions

Excel Formulas

- SUM
- IF
- Percentage
- Subtraction
- Multiplication
- Division
- DATE
- Array
- COUNT
- AVERAGE
- SUMIF
- TRIM
- LEFT, MID, and RIGHT
- VLOOKUP
- RANDOMIZE

1. SUM

All Excel formulas begin with the equals sign, =, followed by a specific text tag denoting the formula you'd like Excel to perform. The SUM formula in Excel is one of the most basic formulas you can enter into a spreadsheet, allowing you to find the sum (or total) of two or more values. To perform the SUM formula, enter the values you'd like to add together using the format, =SUM(value 1, value 2, etc). The values you enter into the SUM formula can either be actual numbers or equal to the number in a specific cell of your spreadsheet.

- To find the SUM of 30 and 80, for example, type the following formula into a cell of your spreadsheet: =SUM(30, 80). Press "Enter," and the cell will produce the total of both numbers: 110.
- To find the SUM of the values in cells B2 and B11, for example, type the following formula into a cell of your spreadsheet: =SUM(B2, B11). Press "Enter," and the cell will produce the total of the numbers currently filled in cells B2 and B11. If there are no numbers in either cell, the formula will return 0.

Keep in mind you can also find the total value of a list of numbers in Excel. To find the SUM of the values in cells B2 through B11, type the following formula into a cell of your spreadsheet: =SUM(B2:B11). Note the colon between both cells, rather than a comma.

2. IF

The IF formula in Excel is denoted =IF(logical_test, value_if_true, value_if_false). This allows you to enter a text value into the cell "if" something else in your spreadsheet is true or false. For example, =IF(D2="Gryffindor", "10", "0") would award 10 points to cell D2 if that cell contained the word "Gryffindor."

There are times when we want to know how many times a value appears in our spreadsheets. But there are also those times when we want to find the cells that contain those values, and input specific data next to them.

We'll go back to Sprung's example for this one. If we want to award 10 points to everyone who belongs in the Gryffindor house, instead of manually typing in 10's next to each Gryffindor student's name, we'll use the IF-THEN formula to say: If the student is in Gryffindor, then he or she should get ten points.

- **The Formula:** IF(logical_test, value_if_true, value_if_false)
- **Logical_Test:** The logical test is the "IF" part of the statement. In this case, the logic is D2="Gryffindor." Make sure your Logical_Test value is in quotation marks.
- **Value_If_True:** If the value is true, that is, if the student lives in Gryffindor, this value is the one that we want to be displayed. In this case, we want it to be the number 10, to indicate that the student was awarded the 10 points. Note: Only use quotation marks if you want the result to be text instead of a number.
- **Value_If_False:** If the value is false and the student does not live in Gryffindor, we want the cell to show "0," for 0 points.

3. Percentage

To perform the percentage formula in Excel, enter the cells you're finding a percentage for in the format, =A1/B1. To convert the resulting decimal value to a percentage, highlight the cell, click the Home tab, and select "Percentage" from the numbers dropdown.

There isn't an Excel "formula" for percentages per se, but Excel makes it easy to convert the value of any cell into a percentage so you're not stuck calculating and reentering the numbers yourself.

The basic setting to convert a cell's value into a percentage is under Excel's Home tab. Select this tab, highlight the cell(s) you'd like to convert to a percentage, and click into the dropdown menu next to Conditional Formatting (this menu button might say "General" at first). Then, select "Percentage" from the list of options that appears. This will convert the value of each cell you've highlighted into a percentage.

Keep in mind if you're using other formulas, such as the division formula (denoted =A1/B1), to return new values, your values might show up as decimals by default. Simply highlight your cells before or after you perform this formula, and set these cells' format to "Percentage" from the Home tab.

4. Subtraction

To perform the subtraction formula in Excel, enter the cells you're subtracting in the format, =SUM(A1, -B1). This will subtract a cell using the SUM formula by adding a negative sign before the cell you're subtracting. For example, if A1 was 10 and B1 was 6, =SUM(A1, -B1) would perform 10 + -6, returning a value of 4.

Like percentages, subtracting doesn't have its formula in Excel either, but that doesn't mean it can't be done. You can subtract any values (or those values inside cells) in two different ways.

- Using the =SUM formula. To subtract multiple values from one another, enter the cells you'd like to subtract in the format =SUM(A1, -B1), with a negative sign (denoted with a hyphen) before the cell whose value you're subtracting. Press enter to return the difference between both cells included in the parentheses. See how this looks in the screenshot above.

- Using the format, =A1-B1. To subtract multiple values from one another, simply type an equals sign followed by your first value or cell, a hyphen, and the value or cell you're subtracting. Press Enter to return the difference between both values.

5. Multiplication

To perform the multiplication formula in Excel, enter the cells you're multiplying in the format, =A1*B1. This formula uses an asterisk to multiply cell A1 by cell B1. For example, if A1 was 10 and B1 was 6, =A1*B1 would return a value of 60.

You might think multiplying values in Excel has its formula or uses the "x" character to denote multiplication between multiple values. It's as easy as an asterisk -- *.

To multiply two or more values in an Excel spreadsheet, highlight an empty cell. Then, enter the values or cells you want to multiply together in the format, =A1*B1*C1 ... etc. The asterisk will effectively multiply each value included in the formula.

Press Enter to return your desired product.

6. Division

To perform the division formula in Excel, enter the cells you're dividing in the format, =A1/B1. This formula uses a forward slash, "/," to divide cell A1 by cell B1. For example, if A1 was 5 and B1 was 10, =A1/B1 would return a decimal value of 0.5.

Division in Excel is one of the simplest functions you can perform. To do so, highlight an empty cell, enter an equals sign, "=," and follow it up with the two (or more) values you'd like to divide with a forward slash, "/," in between. The result should be in the following format: =B2/A2. Hit Enter and your desired quotient should appear in the cell you initially highlighted.

7. DATE

The Excel DATE formula is denoted =DATE(year, month, day). This formula will return a date that corresponds to the values entered in the parentheses -- even values referred from other cells. For example, if A1 was 2018, B1 was 7, and C1 was 11, =DATE(A1, B1, C1) would return 7/11/2018.

Creating dates in the cells of an Excel spreadsheet can be a fickle task now and then. Luckily, there's a handy formula to make formatting your dates easy. There are two ways to use this formula:

- Create dates from a series of cell values. To do this, highlight an empty cell, enter "=DATE," and in parentheses, enter the cells whose values create your desired date, starting with the year, then the month number, then the day. The final format should look like this: =DATE(year, month, day).

- Automatically set today's date. To do this, highlight an empty cell and enter the following string of text: =DATE(YEAR(TODAY()), MONTH(TODAY()), DAY(TODAY())). Pressing enter will return the current date you're working in your Excel spreadsheet.

In either usage of Excel's date formula, your returned date should be in the form of "mm/dd/yy", unless your Excel program is formatted differently.

8. Array

Array formula in Excel surrounds a simple formula in brace characters using the format, {=(Start Value 1:End Value 1)*(Start Value 2:End Value 2)}. By pressing ctrl+shift+center, this will calculate and return value from multiple ranges, rather than just individual cells added to or multiplied by one another.

Calculating the sum, product, or quotient of individual cells is easy just use the =SUM formula and enter the cells, values, or range of cells you want to perform that arithmetic on. But what about multiple ranges? How do you find the combined value of a large group of cells?

Numerical arrays are a useful way to perform more than one formula at the same time in a single cell so you can see one final sum, difference, product, or quotient. If you're looking to find total sales revenue from several sold units, for example, the array formula in Excel is perfect for you. Here's how you'd do it:

- To start using the array formula, type "=SUM," and in parentheses, enter the first of two (or three, or four) ranges of cells you'd like to multiply together. Here's what your progress might look like: =SUM(C2:C5

- Next, add an asterisk after the last cell of the first range you included in your formula. This stands for multiplication. Following this asterisk, enter your second range of cells. You'll be multiplying this second range of cells by the first. Your progress in this formula should now look like this: =SUM(C2:C5*D2:D5)

- Ready to press Enter? Not so fast ... Because this formula is so complicated, Excel reserves a different keyboard command for arrays. Once you've closed the parentheses on your array formula, press Ctrl+Shift+Enter. This will recognize your formula as an array, wrapping your formula in brace characters and successfully returning your product of both ranges combined.

In revenue calculations, this can cut down on your time and effort significantly.

9. COUNT

The COUNT formula in Excel is denoted =COUNT(Start Cell: End Cell). This formula will return a value that is equal to the number of entries found within your desired range of cells. For example, if there are eight cells with entered values between A1 and A10, =COUNT(A1:A10) will return a value of 8.

The COUNT formula in Excel is particularly useful for large spreadsheets, wherein you want to see how many cells contain actual entries. Don't be fooled: This formula won't do any math on the values of the cells themselves. This formula is simply to find out how many cells in a selected range are occupied with something.

10. AVERAGE

To perform the average formula in Excel, enter the values, cells, or range of cells of which you're calculating the average in the format, =AVERAGE(number1, number2, etc.) or =AVERAGE(Start Value: End Value). This will calculate the average of all the values or range of cells included in the parentheses.

Finding the average of a range of cells in Excel keeps you from having to find individual sums and then performing a separate division equation on your total. Using =AVERAGE as your initial text entry, you can let Excel do all the work for you.

For reference, the average of a group of numbers is equal to the sum of those numbers, divided by the number of items in that group.

11. SUMIF

The SUMIF formula in Excel is denoted =SUMIF(range, criteria, [sum range]). This will return the sum of the values within a desired range of cells that all meet one criterion. For example, =SUMIF(C3:C12,">70,000") would return the sum of values between cells C3 and C12 from only the cells that are greater than 70,000.

Let's say you want to determine the profit you generated from a list of leads who are associated with specific area codes or calculate the sum of certain employees' salaries but only if they fall above a particular amount. Doing that manually sounds a bit time-consuming, to say the least.

With the SUMIF function, it doesn't have to be you can easily add up the sum of cells that meet certain criteria.

- **The formula:** =SUMIF(range, criteria, [sum_range])
- **Range:** The range that is being tested using your criteria.
- **Criteria:** The criteria that determine which cells in Criteria_range1 will be added together
- **[Sum_range]:** An optional range of cells you're going to add up in addition to the first Range entered. This field may be omitted.

12. TRIM

The TRIM formula in Excel is denoted =TRIM(text). This formula will remove any spaces entered before and after the text is entered in the cell. For example, if A2 includes the name " Steve Peterson" with unwanted spaces before the first name, =TRIM(A2) would return "Steve Peterson" with no spaces in a new cell.

Email and file sharing are wonderful tools in today's workplace. That is until one of your colleagues sends you a worksheet with some funky spacing. Not only can those rogue spaces make it difficult to search for data, but they also affect the results when you try to add up columns of numbers.

Rather than painstakingly removing and adding spaces as needed, you can clean up any irregular spacing using the TRIM function, which is used to remove extra spaces from data (except for single spaces between words).

- **The formula:** =TRIM(text).
- **Text:** The text or cell from which you want to remove spaces.

Here's an example of how we used the TRIM function to remove extra spaces before a list of names. To do so, we entered =TRIM("A2") into the Formula Bar, and replicated this for each name below it in a new column next to the column with unwanted spaces.

13. LEFT, MID, and RIGHT

Let's say you have a line of text within a cell that you want to break down into a few different segments. Rather than manually retyping each piece of the code into its respective column, users can leverage a series of string functions to deconstruct the sequence as needed: LEFT, MID, or RIGHT.

LEFT

- **Purpose:** Used to extract the first X numbers or characters in a cell.
- **The formula:** =LEFT(text, number_of_characters)
- **Text:** The string that you wish to extract from.
- **Number_of_characters:** The number of characters that you wish to extract starting from the left-most character.

MID

- **Purpose:** Used to extract characters or numbers in the middle based on position.
- **The formula:** =MID(text, start_position, number_of_characters)
- **Text:** The string that you wish to extract from.
- **Start_position:** The position in the string that you want to begin extracting from. For example, the first position in the string is 1.
- **Number_of_characters:** The number of characters that you wish to extract.

RIGHT

- **Purpose:** Used to extract the last X numbers or characters in a cell.
- **The formula:** =RIGHT(text, number_of_characters)
- **Text:** The string that you wish to extract from.
- **Number_of_characters:** The number of characters that you want to extract starting from the right-most character.

14. VLOOKUP

This one is an oldie, but a goodie -- and it's a bit more in-depth than some of the other formulas we've listed here. But it's especially helpful for those times when you have two sets of data on two different spreadsheets and want to combine them into a single spreadsheet.

My colleague, Rachel Sprung -- whose "How to Use Excel" tutorial is a must-read for anyone who wants to learn -- uses a list of names, email addresses, and companies as an example. If you have a list of people's names next to their email addresses in one spreadsheet, and a list of those same people's email addresses next to their company names in the other, but you want the names, email addresses, and company names of those people to appear in one place, that's where VLOOKUP comes in.

Note: When using this formula, you must be certain that at least one column appears identically in both spreadsheets. Scour your data sets to make sure the column of data you're using to combine your information is the same, including no extra spaces.

The formula: VLOOKUP(lookup value, table array, column number, [range lookup])

Lookup Value: The identical value you have in both spreadsheets. Choose the first value in your first spreadsheet. In Sprung's example that follows, this means the first email address on the list, or cell 2 (C2).

Table Array: The range of columns on Sheet 2 you're going to pull your data from, including the column of data identical to your lookup value (in our example, email addresses) in Sheet 1 as well as the column of data you're trying to copy to Sheet 1. In our example, this is "Sheet2!A: B." "A" means Column A in Sheet 2, which is the column in Sheet 2 where the data identical to our lookup value (email) in Sheet 1 is listed. The "B" means Column B, which contains the information that's only available in Sheet 2 that you want to translate to Sheet 1.

Column Number: The table array tells Excel where (which column) the new data you want to copy to Sheet 1 is located. In our example, this would be the "House" column, the second one in our table array, making it column number 2.

Range Lookup: Use FALSE to ensure you pull in only exact value matches.

15. RANDOMIZE

There's a great article that likens Excel's RANDOMIZE formula to shuffling a deck of cards. The entire deck is a column, and each card, 52 in a deck, is a row. "To shuffle the deck," writes Steve McDonnell, "you can compute a new column of data, populate each cell in the column with a random number, and sort the workbook based on the random number field."

In marketing, you might use this feature when you want to assign a random number to a list of contacts, like if you wanted to experiment with a new email campaign and had to use blind criteria to select who would receive it. By assigning numbers to said contacts, you could apply the rule, "Any contact with a figure of 6 or above will be added to the new campaign."

The formula: RAND()

Start with a single column of contacts. Then, in the column adjacent to it, type "RAND()", without the quotation marks, starting with the top contact's row.

For the example below: RANDBETWEEN(bottom, top)

- **RANDBETWEEN** allows you to dictate the range of numbers that you want to be assigned. In the case of this example, I wanted to use one through 10.
- **Bottom:** The lowest number in the range.
- **Top:** The highest number in the range,

How To Insert Formula In Excel For Entire Column

To insert a formula in Excel for an entire column of your spreadsheet, enter the formula into the topmost cell of your desired column and press "Enter." Then, highlight and double-click the bottom-right corner of this cell to copy the formula into every cell below it in the column.

Sometimes, you might want to run the same formula across an entire row or column of your spreadsheet. Let's say, for example, you have a list of numbers in columns A and B of a spreadsheet and want to enter individual totals of each row into column C.

It would be too tedious to adjust the values of the formula for each cell so you're finding the total of each row's respective numbers. Luckily, Excel allows you to automatically compete for the column; all you have to do is enter the formula in the first row. Check out the following steps:

- Type your formula into an empty cell and press "Enter" to run the formula.SUM formula entered in column C of Excel spreadsheet to find the sum of cells B2 and C2.
- Hover your cursor over the bottom-right corner of the cell containing the formula. You'll see a small, bold "+" symbol appear.
- While you can double-click this symbol to automatically fill the entire column with your formula, you can also click and drag your cursor down manually to fill only a specific length of the column. insert-formula-in-excel-for-entire-column once you've reached the last cell in the column you'd like to enter your formula, release your mouse to copy the formula. Then, simply check each new value to ensure it corresponds to the correct cells.

Five Time-Saving Ways To Insert Data Into Excel

When analyzing data, there are five common ways of inserting basic Excel formulas. Each strategy comes with its advantages. Therefore, before diving further into the main formulas, we'll clarify those methods, so you can create your preferred workflow earlier on.

1. Simple Insertion: Typing A Formula Inside The Cell

Typing a formula in a cell or the formula bar is the most straightforward method of inserting basic Excel formulas. The process usually starts by typing an equal sign, followed by the name of an Excel function.

Excel is quite intelligent in that when you start typing the name of the function, a pop-up function hint will show. It's from this list you'll select your preference. However, don't press the Enter key. Instead, press the Tab key so that you can continue to insert other options. Otherwise, you may find yourself with an invalid name error, often as '#NAME?'. To fix it, just re-select the cell, and go to the formula bar to complete your function.

2. Using Insert Function Option From Formulas Tab

If you want full control of your functions insertion, using the Excel Insert Function dialogue box is all you ever need. To achieve this, go to the Formulas tab and select the first menu labeled Insert Function. The dialogue box will contain all the functions you need to complete your financial analysis.

3. Selecting A Formula From One Of The Groups In Formula Tab

This option is for those who want to delve into their favorite functions quickly. To find this menu, navigate to the Formulas tab and select your preferred group. Click to show a sub-menu filled with a list of functions. From there, you can select your preference. However, if you find your preferred group is not on the tab, click on the More Functions option – it's probably just hidden there.

4. Using AutoSum Option

For quick and everyday tasks, the AutoSum function is your go-to option. So, navigate to the Home tab, in the far-right corner, and click the AutoSum option. Then click the caret to show other hidden formulas. This option is also available in the Formulas tab first option after the Insert Function option.

5. Quick Insert: Use Recently Used Tabs

If you find re-typing your most recent formula a monotonous task, then use the Recently Used menu. It's on the Formulas tab, a third menu option just next to AutoSum.

Excel Keyboard Shortcuts

1. Quickly Select Rows, Columns, Or The Whole Spreadsheet.

Perhaps you're crunched for time. I mean, who isn't? No time, no problem. You can select your entire spreadsheet with just one click. All you have to do is simply click the tab in the top-left corner of your sheet to highlight everything all at once.

Just want to select everything in a particular column of a row? That's just as easy with these shortcuts:

For Mac:

- Select Column = Command + Shift + Down/Up
- Select Row = Command + Shift + Right/Left

For PC:

- Select Column = Control + Shift + Down/Up
- Select Row = Control + Shift + Right/Left

This shortcut is especially helpful when you're working with larger data sets, but only need to select a specific piece of it.

2. Quickly Open, Close, Or Create A Workbook.

Need to open, close, or create a workbook on the fly? The following keyboard shortcuts will enable you to complete any of the above actions in less than a minute.

For Mac:

- Open = Command + O
- Close = Command + W
- Create New = Command + N

For PC:

- Open = Control + O
- Close = Control + F4
- Create New = Control + N

3. Format Numbers Into Currency.

Have raw data that you want to turn into currency? Whether it be salary figures, marketing budgets, or ticket sales for an event, the solution is simple. Just highlight the cells you wish to reformat, and select Control + Shift + $. The numbers will automatically translate into dollar amounts, complete with dollar signs, commas, and decimal points.

Note: This shortcut also works with percentages. If you want to label a column of numerical values as "percent" figures, replace "$" with "%".

4. Insert Current Date And Time Into A Cell.

Whether you're logging social media posts or keeping track of tasks you're checking off your to-do list, you might want to add a date and time stamp to your worksheet. Start by selecting the cell to which you want to add this information.

Then, depending on what you want to insert, do one of the following:

- Insert current date = Control + ; (semi-colon)
- Insert current time = Control + Shift + ; (semi-colon)
- Insert current date and time = Control + ; (semi-colon), SPACE, and then Control + Shift + ; (semi-colon).

CTRL Shortcuts	Functions
CTRL + A	Select All
CTRL + B	Bold
CTRL + C	Copy
CTRL + ALT + V	Paste Special
CTRL + D	Fill Down
CTRL + F	Find
CTRL + G	Go to
CTRL + H	Replace
CTRL + I	Italic
CTRL + K	Insert Hyperlink
CTRL + N	New Workbook
CTRL + O	Open File
CTRL + P	Print
CTRL + R	Fill right
CTRL + S	Save workbook
CTRL + T	Create Table
CTRL + U	Underline
CTRL + V	Paste
CTRL + W	Close window
CTRL + X	Cut
CTRL + Y	Repeat
CTRL + Z	Undo
CTRL + 1	Format Box
CTRL + 5	Strike-through
CTRL + 9	Hide row
SHIFT + CTRL + 9	Unhide row
CTRL + 0	Hide column
SHIFT + CTRL + 0	Unhide column
CTRL + ~	Show formulas/values
CTRL + '	Copy above formula
CTRL + [	Precedents
CTRL +]	Dependents
CTRL + ;	Display date
SHIFT + CTRL + :	Display time
CTRL + Space	Select column
CTRL + Enter	Fill selection w/ entry

Other Excel Tricks

1. Customize The Color Of Your Tabs.

If you've got a ton of different sheets in one workbook, which happens to the best of us, make it easier to identify where you need to go by color-coding the tabs. For example, you might label last month's marketing reports with red, and this month's with orange.

Simply right-click a tab and select "Tab Color." A popup will appear that allows you to choose a color from an existing theme, or customize one to meet your needs.

2. Add A Comment To A Cell.

When you want to make a note or add a comment to a specific cell within a worksheet, simply right-click the cell you want to comment on, then click Insert Comment. Type your comment into the text box, and click outside the comment box to save it.

Cells that contain comments display a small, red triangle in the corner. To view the comment, hover over it.

3. Copy And Duplicate Formatting.

If you've ever spent some time formatting a sheet to your liking, you probably agree that it's not exactly the most enjoyable activity. It's pretty tedious.

For that reason, likely, you don't want to repeat the process next time, nor do you have to. Thanks to Excel's Format Painter, you can easily copy the formatting from one area of a worksheet to another.

Select what you'd like to replicate, then select the Format Painter option, the paintbrush icon, from the dashboard. The pointer will then display a paintbrush, prompting you to select the cell, text, or entire worksheet to which you want to apply that formatting.

4. Identify Duplicate Values.

In many instances, duplicate values, like duplicate content when managing SEO, can be troublesome if gone uncorrected. In some cases, though, you simply need to be aware of it.

Whatever the situation may be, it's easy to surface any existing duplicate values within your worksheet in just a few quick steps. To do so, click into the Conditional Formatting option, and select Highlight Cell Rules > Duplicate Values

Using the popup, create the desired formatting rule to specify which type of duplicate content you wish to bring forward.

In the example above, we were looking to identify any duplicate salaries within the selected range and formatted the duplicate cells in yellow.

In marketing, the use of Excel is pretty inevitable but with these tricks, it doesn't have to be so daunting. As they say, practice makes perfect. The more you use these formulas, shortcuts, and tricks, the more they'll become second nature.

Mistakes To Avoid When Working With Formulas In Excel

Remember the rules of Brackets of Division, Multiplication, Addition, & Subtraction (BODMAS). This means expressions are brackets are evaluated first. For arithmetic operators, the division is evaluated first followed by multiplication then addition and subtraction is the last one to be evaluated. Using this rule, we can rewrite the above formula as =(A2 * D2) / 2. This will ensure that A2 and D2 are first evaluated then divided by two.

Excel spreadsheet formulas usually work with numeric data; you can take advantage of data validation to specify the type of data that should be accepted by a cell i.e. numbers only.

To ensure that you are working with the correct cell addresses referenced in the formulas, you can press F2 on the keyboard. This will highlight the cell addresses used in the formula, and you can cross-check to ensure they are the desired cell addresses.

When you are working with many rows, you can use serial numbers for all the rows and have a record count at the bottom of the sheet. You should compare the serial number count with the record total to ensure that your formulas included all the rows.

CHAPTER 5: MICROSOFT EXCEL COUNTING AND LOGIC'S FUNCTIONS

A function is a predefined formula already available in Excel. Functions streamline the process of creating a calculation

Functions streamline the process of creating a calculation. To date, Excel has more than 500 functions.

So in summary, a formula is any calculation in Excel, but a function is a pre-defined calculation.

For example:

=A1/A2 is just a formula

=MAX(A1:B20) is a formula containing a function.

Definition of Counting Function

It is used to count the number of cells or range containing numbers.

It can also be used to count the number of arguments that contain numbers.

Syntax of Count Function

The syntax of count Function is given below **Count (argument_1, argument_2, argument_3, ... argument_n)**

You can add up to 255 arguments.

Argument_1 – It is a mandatory argument. It can be a cell reference, range of cells or any data to be counted.

Argument_2,Argument_3, ... Argument_n – Except argument_1 all other arguments are optional.

It can also be a cell reference, range of cells or any data to be counted.

Data Sheet It contains number 1 to 20 some in numerical format and some in text format in the range A1:A10 and C1:C10 as shown in the Fig 1.1. Just spend few minutes in Data sheet section provided in all the lessons before proceeding to question part.

	A	B	C	D
1	One		11	
2	2		Twelve	
3	3		13	
4	4		14	
5	Five		15	
6	6		Sixteen	
7	7		17	
8	Eight		18	
9	9		Nineteen	
10	10		20	

Cell reference: B10

CountIf Function

It is used to count the number of cells or range which meets the given criteria. It can also be used to count the number of arguments which meets the given criteria.

Syntax of Count Function

The syntax of countif Function is given below

Count (range,criteria)

Range: It can be a cell reference, range of cells or any data to be counted. It defines the range of cells to be evaluated by criteria.

Criteria: It can be Logical condition, numerical condition, cell reference or string which determine the cells to be counted.

Data Sheet

It contains the data of average temperature in Day and Night of each month in 2020.

Using this data sheet, we'll learn how to effectively use the Countif function to count the data with specified condition.

	A	B	C
1	Month	Temperature in Day time(°C)	Temperature in Night Time(°C)
2	January	35	29
3	February	33	29
4	March	34	28
5	April	35	27
6	May	32	27
7	June	29	26
8	July	29	25
9	August	28	26
10	September	27	25
11	October	30	28
12	November	31	28
13	December	30	30

Sum Function

It is used to add all number in a range of cells and return the result.

Syntax of Sum Function

The syntax of sum Function is given below

Sum(number_1,[number_2,...number_n])

Number_1(mandatory)- It indicate numbers or cell reference or cell range.

Number_2,number_3,..(Optional) – It also indicates numbers or cell reference or cell range.

Data Sheet

It contains the data of marks secured by 10 students in mathematics, English and science subjects. Using this data sheet, we'll learn how to effectively use the sum function to add marks.

	A	B	C	D	E
1	S.No	Student Name	Maths	English	Science
2	1	Constance Hopkins	80	59	69
3	2	Kerry Long	86	60	59
4	3	Raul Black	86	87	81
5	4	Willis Jacobs	75	98	86
6	5	Lindsay Mathis	84	68	72
7	6	Becky Cain	95	84	94
8	7	Shawna Ellis	100	82	76
9	8	Alexander Underwood	70	73	85
10	9	Mike Carlson	66	76	96
11	10	Brandy Lopez	59	68	85
12					

Sumif Function

Definition of Sumif Function

It is used to add numbers in cells or range which meets the given criteria.

Syntax of Count Function

The syntax of Sumif Function is given below

Sumif (range, criteria, [Sum range])

Range(Mandatory)- It can be a cell reference, range of cells or any data to be added. It defines the range of cells to be evaluated by criteria.

Criteria(Mandatory) – It can be Logical condition, numerical condition, cell reference or string which determine the cells to be added.

Sum Range(Optional)- It defines the actual cell or range to add. If this parameter is omitted then excel take the first parameter (Range) for evaluation.

Let us see what will be considered as an actual range by Excel when there is a contradiction between Range and Sum Range.

Range Value	Sum Range Value	Actual Range for calculation
A1:A20	B1:B10	B1:B20
A1:B20	C1:D20	C1:D20
A1:B20	C1:C20	C1:D20
A1:A10	C1:D20	C1:C20
A1:A15	C1:D20	C1:C15

Definition of IF function

Job of IF function is to check whether the given conditions met and then it returns one value if the condition is true or another value if the condition is false. However, it should return only one value at a time. You can nest the IF statement but excel allows you to nest up to 64 levels. It will throw an error #Name? if the condition or expression to be evaluate is invalid.

Syntax of Excel IF function

The syntax of IF function is given below

IF (logical_test, value_if_true, value_if_false)

It accepts three arguments where the first one is mandatory and remaining two are optional.

Logical_test- This is the first argument of excel IF function and in this argument user has to give an expression or condition to be evaluated. It allow user to use text value, number, date or any arithmetic operator such as +, -, * etc.

Value_if_true (Optional)- This is the second argument and excel return the value specified in this argument if the condition or expression given in the first argument is true.

If you don't want to return anything then you can simply skip it by leaving it blank or use "".

If you just want to return TRUE then you need to specify TRUE inside the double quotes.

If you want to perform any arithmetic calculation then you can specify the formula you need.

Value_if_false(Optional)-This is the third argument and excel return the value specified in this argument if the condition or expression given in the first argument is false.

If you do not want to return anything then you can simply skip it by leaving it blank or use "".

If you just want to return FALSE then you need to specify FALSE inside the double quotes.

If you want to perform any arithmetic calculation then you can specify the formula you need.

Let us move on to the practical examples to explore more

Definition of AND function

AND function return true when all the conditions in the AND function is true. It return false when one or more conditions become false. Be remember that AND function return either TRUE or FALSE and it will not return any other values.

Syntax of Excel AND function

The syntax of AND function is given below

AND (Condition 1, Condition 2,......)

Condition 1 (Mandatory) - This is the first condition to check and it return either true or false

Condition 2 (Optional) –All the conditions other than first condition are all optional. It also returns either true or false. You can add up to maximum of 30 conditions.

Definition of OR function

ORfunction return true when any of the conditions are true. It return false when all the conditions become false. It returns either TRUE or FALSE and it will not return any other values.

Syntax of Excel OR function

The syntax of OR function is given below

OR (Condition 1, Condition 2,......)

Condition 1 (Mandatory) - This is the first condition to check and it return either true or false

Condition 2 (Optional) –All the conditions other than first condition are all optional. It also returns either true or false.

You can add up to maximum of 30 conditions.

Definition of NOT function

NOT function return TRUE when condition become FALSE and return FALSE when

condition become TRUE.

Syntax of NOT function

The syntax of NOT function is given below

NOT (Logical_value)

Logical_Value- It denotes the logical expression or value

Definition of EVEN function

EVEN Function converts any Even number or any number into the nearest even number. The selected number can be a whole number or in decimal. The important thing is, if we feed an even number, then it will not be changed, and it only considers numbers.

Syntax of EVEN function

EVEN(number)

number : a valid number. Can be decimal

Notes:

1. The formula only works with numbers.

2. The formula returns the nearest next EVEN integer given input any decimal number.

3. The function returns the number away from zero.

4. No argument to the function returns 0 as result, so do check all the blank cell.

5. The function returns #VALUE! Error if the number is non numeric.

Definition of ODD function

ODD Function converts any Odd number or any number into the nearest odd number. The selected number can be a whole number or in decimal. The important thing is, if we feed an odd number, then it will not be changed, and it only considers numbers.

Syntax of ODD function

ODD(number)

number : a valid number. Can be decimal

Notes:

1. The formula only works with numbers.

2. The formula returns the nearest next ODD integer given input any decimal number.

3. The function returns the number away from zero.

4. No argument to the function returns 0 as result, so do check all the blank cell.

5. The function returns #VALUE! Error if the number is non numeric.

CHAPTER 6: MICROSOFT EXCEL FUNCTIONS OF DATE AND TIME

Excel Date and Time functions can be used to extract information from, and perform operations on, Excel Dates and Times. Some of the Excel Date & Time functions are new to Excel 2016 or Excel 2019, so are not available in earlier versions of Excel. You can find this information in the applicability section of the function.

How To Insert The Current Date And Time In Excel?

For anyone working as a financial analyst, it can be useful to insert the current time and date into an Excel spreadsheet. This guide will break down how the Excel current date and time function works and outline situations where it will be helpful in your analysis.

Excel Current Date and Time Formulas (Dynamic)

There are two formulas to use, depending on what type of information you're looking to insert in your spreadsheet. Note: These are dynamic formulas and will update whenever a spreadsheet is opened.

Current date formula:

=TODAY()

Current time formula:

=NOW()

Excel Current Date And Time Example

Let's look at a real example in an Excel spreadsheet of how these two formulas work. In the screenshot below, you can see how each works and what the corresponding output is. For example, if, at the time of creating the formula, it's May 24, 2018, at 1:36 p.m., then the following information will appear in your spreadsheet. **Note:** Excel uses a 24-hour clock when it outputs the time.

Excel Current Date And Time

As you can see, the =TODAY() formula only includes the day, month, and year. The =NOW() function displays more information, showing the day, month, year, hour, and minutes (using a 24-hour clock).

Excel Current Date And Time Formulas (Static)

You may not always want the figures in the file to update every time you open the file. If this is the case, then you'll want to insert a static version of the formulas.

Static Formulas Are:

- "Ctrl +;" – inserts the date (Windows)
- "Ctrl + Shift +;" – inserts the date and time (Windows)
- "COMMAND +;" (Mac)

Why Insert The Current Date And Time In Excel?

There are many reasons you may want to display the current date and time in Excel. Let's say that you want users to have the current time displayed on a cover page every time you print off a financial model.

Reasons To Include Time And Date Include:

- Creating an activity log
- On a cover page
- When printing a document
- For version control
- When showing time-sensitive information
- When discounting cash flows to the present (Net Present Value and XNPV function)

How To Change The Date And Time Formatting

You may wish to change the format of the date or time displayed in the spreadsheet. To do this, press F1 (or right-click on the cell and click Format Cells). Once you see the Format Cells box appear on the screen, you can click on Number and then select Date or Time and choose the formatting you want to appear in your spreadsheet.

Applications In Financial Modeling

The Excel current time and date function are very useful in performing financial analysis, as time is a critical factor in financial modeling and valuation. The most important use is in discounting cash flows and ensuring that the net present value date is correct. You may wish to use a static or dynamic version of the formulas shown in this article, depending on the analysis being performed.

Date And Time Functions

The following table lists all the Date & Time functions & Description:

- **DATE:** Returns the serial number of a particular date.
- **DATEDIF:** Calculates the number of days, months, or years between two dates.

- **DATEVALUE:** Converts a date in the form of text to a serial number.

- **DAY:** Converts a serial number to a day of the month.

- **DAYS:** Returns the number of days between two dates.

- **DAYS360:** Calculates the number of days between two dates, based on a 360-day year.

- **EDATE:** Returns the serial number of the date that is the indicated number of months before or after the start date.

- **EOMONTH:** Returns the serial number of the last day of the month before or after a specified number of months.

- **HOUR:** Converts a serial number to an hour.

- **ISOWEEKNUM:** Returns the number of the ISO week number of the year for a given date.

- **MINUTE:** Converts a serial number to a minute.

- **MONTH:** Converts a serial number to a month.

- **NETWORKDAYS:** Returns the number of whole workdays between two dates.

- **NETWORKDAYS.INTL:** Returns the number of whole workdays between two dates (international version).

- **NOW:** Returns the serial number of the current date and time.

- **SECOND:** Converts a serial number to a second.

- **TIME:** Returns the serial number of a particular time.

- **TIME VALUE:** Converts a time in the form of text to a serial number.

- **TODAY:** Returns the serial number of today's date.

- **WEEKDAY:** Converts a serial number to a day of the week.

- **WEEKNUM:** Returns the week number in the year.

- **WORKDAY:** Returns the serial number of the date before or after a specified number of workdays.

- **WORKDAY.INTL:** After a specified number of workdays using parameters to indicate which and how many days are weekend days.

- **YEAR:** Converts a serial number to a year.

- **YEARFRAC:** Returns the year fraction representing the number of whole days between start_date and end_date.

CHAPTER 7: PIVOT TABLE IN MICROSOFT EXCEL

PivotTable is an extremely powerful tool that you can use to slice and dice data. In this tutorial, you will learn these PivotTable features in detail along with examples. By the time you complete this tutorial, you will have sufficient knowledge on PivotTable features that can get you started with exploring, analyzing, and reporting data based on the requirements.

A PivotTable is an extremely powerful tool that you can use to slice and dice data. You can track and analyze hundreds of thousands of data points with a compact table that can be changed dynamically to enable you to find the different perspectives of the data. It is a simple tool to use, yet powerful.

The Major Features Of A Pivottable Are As Follows:

- Creating a PivotTable is extremely simple and fast
- Enabling churning of data instantly by simple dragging of fields, sorting and filtering, and different calculations on the data.
- Arriving at the suitable representation for your data as you gain insights into it.
- Ability to create reports on the fly.
- Producing multiple reports from the same PivotTable in a matter of seconds
- Providing interactive reports to synchronize with the audience.

You can create a PivotTable either from a range of data or from an Excel table. In both cases, the first row of the data should contain the headers for the columns. If you are sure of the fields to be included in the PivotTable and the layout you want to have, you can start with an empty PivotTable and construct the PivotTable. In case you are not sure which PivotTable layout is best suitable for your data, you can make use of Recommended PivotTables command of Excel to view the PivotTables customized to your data and choose the one you like.

Excel Pivot Tables - Creation

Creating Pivottable

To create a PivotTable from this data range, do the following:

- Ensure that the first row has headers. You need headers because they will be the field names in your PivotTable.
- Name the data range as SalesData_Range.
- Click on the data range – SalesData_Range.

- Click the INSERT tab on the Ribbon.

Click PivotTable in the Tables group. The Create PivotTable dialog box appears.

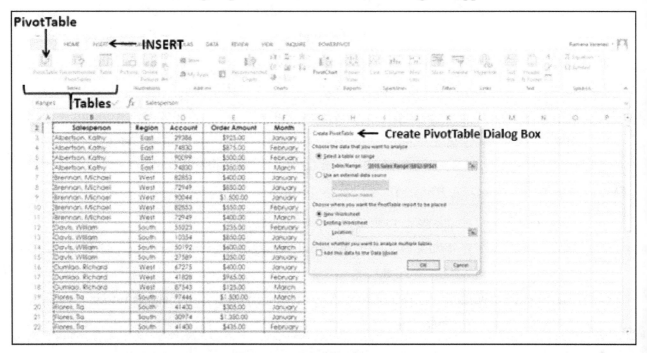

In Create PivotTable dialog box, under Choose the data that you want to analyze, you can either select a Table or Range from the current workbook or use an external data source.

As you are creating a PivotTable from a data range, select the following from the dialog box:

- Select Select a table or range.
- In the Table/Range box, type the range name – SalesData_Range.
- Select New Worksheet under Choose where you want the PivotTable report to be placed and click OK.

You can choose to analyze multiple tables, by adding this data range to Data Model. You can learn how to analyze multiple tables, use of Data Model, and how to use an external data source to create a PivotTable in the tutorial Excel PowerPivot.

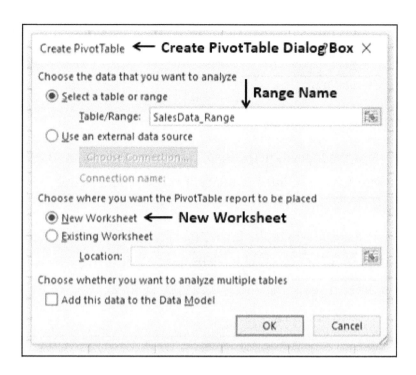

A new worksheet is inserted into your workbook. The new worksheet contains an empty Pivot Table. Name the worksheet – Range-PivotTable.

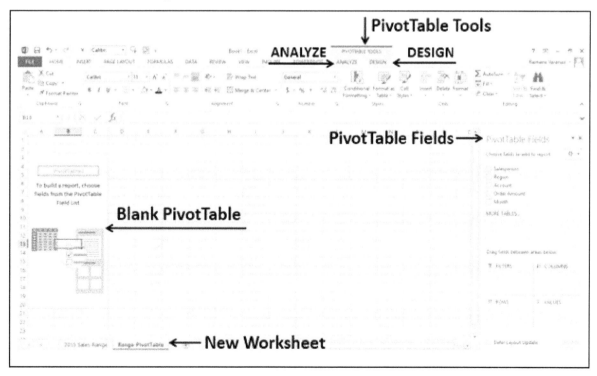

As you can observe, the PivotTable Fields list appears on the right side of the worksheet, containing the header names of the columns in the data range. Further, on the Ribbon, PivotTable Tools – ANALYZE and DESIGN appear.

Adding Fields To The Pivottable

For now, observe the steps to add fields to the PivotTable. Suppose you want to summarize the order amount salesperson-wise for the months January, February, and March. You can do it in a few simple steps as follows:

- Click on the field Salesperson in the PivotTable Fields list and drag it to the ROWS area.
- Click the field Month in the PivotTable Fields list and drag that also to the ROWS area.
- Click on Order Amount and drag it to $\sum$ the VALUES area.

Your first PivotTable is ready as shown below

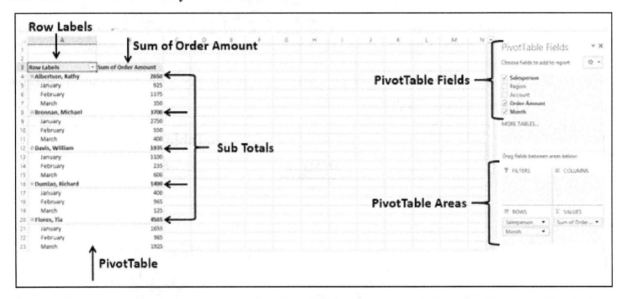

Observe that two columns appear in the PivotTable, one containing the Row Labels that you selected, i.e. Salesperson and Month, and a second one containing Sum of Order Amount. In addition to the Sum of Order Amount month-wise for each Salesperson, you will also get subtotals representing the total sales by that person. If you scroll down the worksheet, you will find the last row as Grand Total representing total sales. You will learn more about producing PivotTables as per the need as you progress through this tutorial.

Creating A Pivottable From A Table

Consider the following Excel table that contains the same sales data as in the previous section:

	A	B	C	D	E	F
1						
2		Salesperson	Region	Account	Order Amount	Month
3		Albertson, Kathy	East	29386	$925.00	January
4		Albertson, Kathy	East	74830	$875.00	February
5		Albertson, Kathy	East	90099	$500.00	February
6		Albertson, Kathy	East	74830	$350.00	March
7		Brennan, Michael	West	82853	$400.00	January
8		Brennan, Michael	West	72949	$850.00	January
9		Brennan, Michael	West	90044	$1,500.00	January
10		Brennan, Michael	West	82853	$550.00	February
11		Brennan, Michael	West	72949	$400.00	March
12		Davis, William	South	55223	$235.00	February
13		Davis, William	South	10354	$850.00	January
14		Davis, William	South	50192	$600.00	March
15		Davis, William	South	27589	$250.00	January
16		Dumlao, Richard	West	67275	$400.00	January
17		Dumlao, Richard	West	41828	$965.00	February
18		Dumlao, Richard	West	87543	$125.00	March
19		Flores, Tia	South	97446	$1,500.00	March
20		Flores, Tia	South	41400	$305.00	January
21		Flores, Tia	South	30974	$1,350.00	January
22		Flores, Tia	South	41400	$435.00	February
23		Flores, Tia	South	30974	$550.00	February

2015 Sales Range   Range-PivotTable   2015 Sales Table   (+)

An Excel table will inherently have a name and the columns will have headers, which is a requirement to create a PivotTable. Suppose the table name is SalesData_Table. To create a PivotTable from this Excel table, do the following:

- Click on the table – SalesData_Table.
- Click the INSERT tab on the Ribbon.
- Click PivotTable in the Tables group. The Create PivotTable dialog box appears.

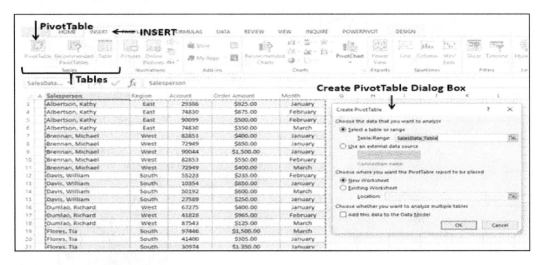

- Click Select a table or range.
- In the Table/Range box, type the table name, SalesData_Table.
- Select New Worksheet under Choose where you want the PivotTable report to be placed. Click OK.

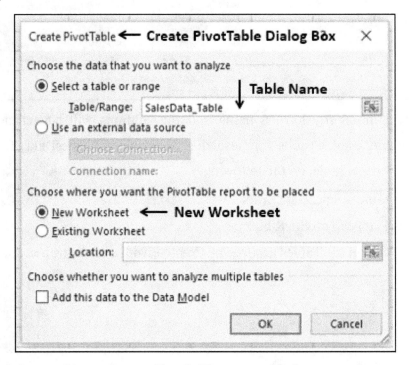

A new worksheet is inserted into your workbook. The new worksheet contains an empty Pivot Table. Name the worksheet – Table-PivotTable. The worksheet – Table-PivotTable looks similar to the one you have got in the data range case in the earlier section. You can add fields to the PivotTable as you have seen in the section – Adding Fields to the PivotTable.

Creating A Pivottable With Recommended Pivottables

In case you are not familiar with Excel PivotTables or if you do not know which fields would result in a meaningful report, you can use the Recommended PivotTables command in Excel. Recommended PivotTables gives you all the possible reports with your data along with the associated layout. In other words, the options displayed will be the PivotTables that are customized to your data.

To create a PivotTable from the Excel table SalesData-Table using Recommended PivotTables, proceed as follows:

- Click on the table SalesData-Table.
- Click the INSERT tab.
- Click Recommended PivotTables in the Tables group. The Recommended PivotTables Dialog Box appears.

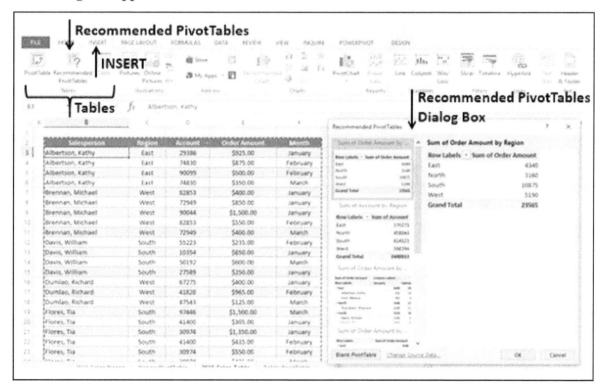

Recommended PivotTables

In the Recommended PivotTables dialog box, the possible customized PivotTables that suit your data will be displayed.

- Click on each of the PivotTable options to see the preview on the right side.
- Click on the PivotTable - Sum of Order Amount by Salesperson and Month and click OK.

You will get the preview on the right side.

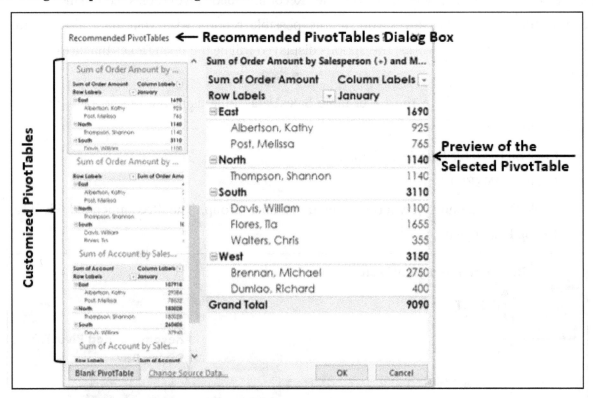

The selected PivotTable appears on a new worksheet in your workbook.

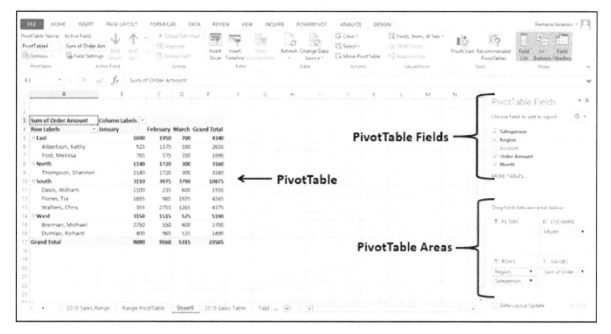

- You can see that the PivotTable Fields - Salesperson, Region, Order Amount, and Month got selected. Of these, Region and Salesperson are in ROWS area, Month is in COLUMNS area, and Sum of Order Amount is in $\sum$ VALUES area.
- The PivotTable summarized the data Region-wise, Salesperson-wise, and Month-wise. The subtotals are displayed for each Region, each Salesperson, and each Month.

Excel Pivot Tables - Fields

PivotTable Fields is a Task Pane associated with a PivotTable. The PivotTable Fields Task Pane comprises Fields and Areas. By default, the Task Pane appears at the right side of the window with Fields displayed above Areas. Fields represent the columns in your data range or Excel table and will have checkboxes.

The selected fields are displayed in the report. Areas represent the layout of the report and the calculations included in the report. At the bottom of the Task Pane, you will find an option – Defer Layout Update with an UPDATE button next to it:

- By default, this is not selected and whatever changes you make in the selection of fields or the layout options are reflected in the PivotTable instantly.
- If you select this, the changes in your selections are not updated until you click on the UPDATE button.

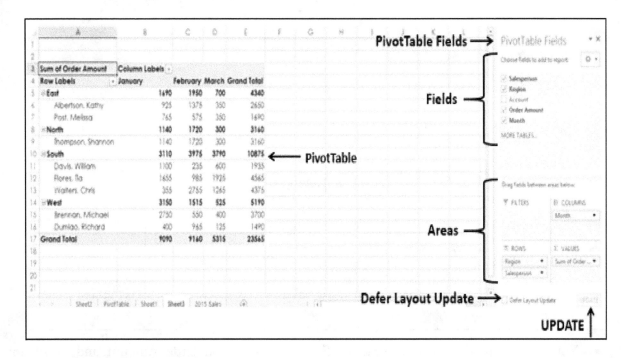

PivotTable Fields Task Pane

You can find the PivotTable Fields Task Pane on the worksheet where you have a PivotTable. To view the PivotTable Fields Task Pane, click the PivotTable. In case the PivotTable Fields Task Pane is not displayed, check the Ribbon for the following:

- Click the ANALYZE tab under PivotTable Tools on the Ribbon.
- Check if Fields List is selected (i.e. highlighted) in the Show group.
- If Fields List is not selected, then click it.
- The PivotTable Fields Task Pane will be displayed on the right side of the window, with the title – PivotTable Fields.

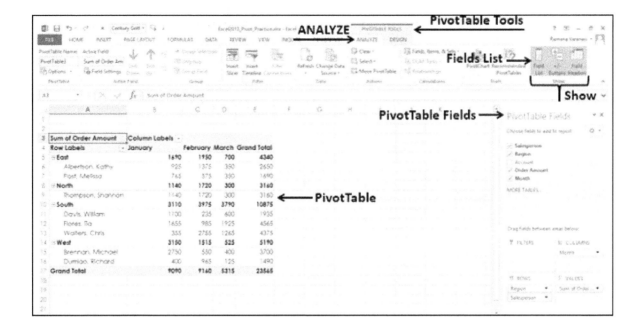

Moving PivotTable Fields Task Pane

On the right of the title PivotTable Fields of the PivotTable Task Pane, you will find the button Down Arrow. This represents Task Pane Options. Click the button Down Arrow. The Task Pane Options-Move, Size, and Close appear in the dropdown list.

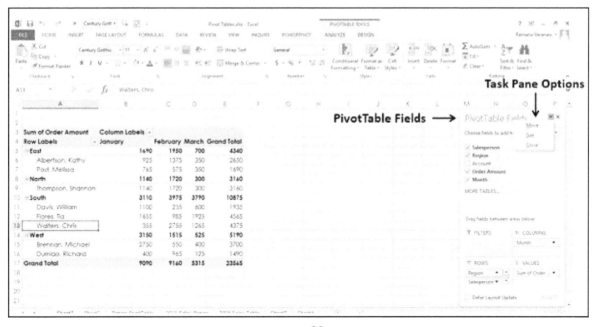

You can move the PivotTables Task Pane to anywhere you want in the window as follows:

- Click Move in the dropdown list. The 4 Directional Arrow button appears on the Task Pane.
- Click the 4 Directional Arrow icon and drag the pane to a position where you want to place it. You can place the TaskPane next to the PivotTable as given below.

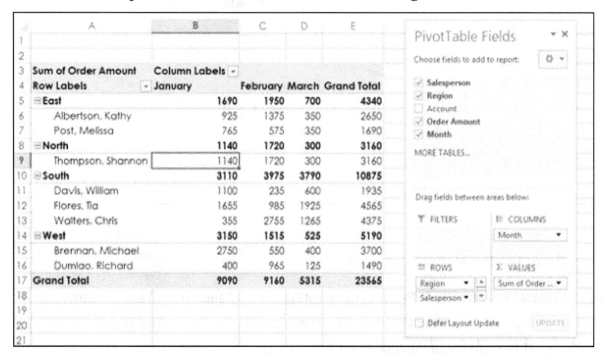

- You can place the Task Pane on the left side of the window as given below.

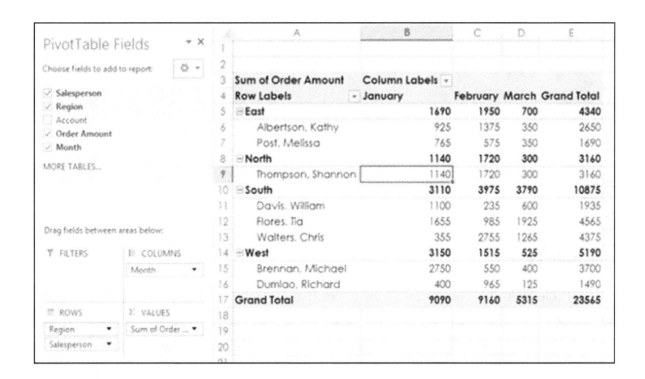

Sum of Order Amount	Column Labels				
Row Labels	January	February	March	Grand Total	
East	1690	1950	700	4340	
Albertson, Kathy	925	1375	350	2650	
Post, Melissa	765	575	350	1690	
North	1140	1720	300	3160	
Thompson, Shannon	1140	1720	300	3160	
South	3110	3975	3790	10875	
Davis, William	1100	235	600	1935	
Flores, Tia	1655	985	1925	4565	
Walters, Chris	355	2755	1265	4375	
West	3150	1515	525	5190	
Brennan, Michael	2750	550	400	3700	
Dumlao, Richard	400	965	125	1490	
Grand Total	9090	9160	5315	23565	

Resizing PivotTable Fields Task Pane

You can resize the PivotTables Task Pane – i.e. increase / decrease the Task Pane length and/or width as follows:

- Click on Task Pane Options – Down Arrow that is on the right side of the title - PivotTable Fields.
- Click on Size in the dropdown list.
- Use the symbol ⇔ to increase/decrease the width of the Task Pane.
- Use the symbol ⇕ to increase/decrease the width of the Task Pane.
- In the ∑ VALUES area, to make the Sum of Order Amount visible completely, you can resize the Task Pane as given below.

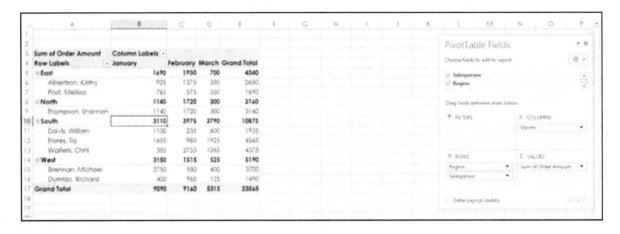

PivotTable Fields

The PivotTable Fields list comprises all the tables that are associated with your workbook and the corresponding fields. It is by selecting the fields in the PivotTable fields list, you will create the PivotTable. The tables and the corresponding fields with checkboxes, reflect your PivotTable data. As you can check/uncheck the fields randomly, you can quickly change the PivotTable, highlighting the summarized data that you want to report or present.

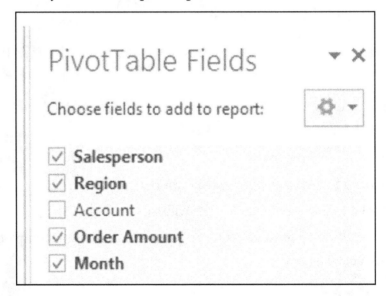

As you can observe, if there is only one table, the table name will not be displayed in the PivotTable Fields list. Only the fields will be displayed with checkboxes. Above the fields list, you will find the action Choose fields to add to the report. To the right, you will find the button – Settings that represents Tools.

Click on the Tools button.

In the dropdown list, you will find the following:

- Five different layout options for Fields and Areas.
- Two options for the Sort order of the fields in the Fields list:
- Sort A to Z.
- Sort in Data Source Order.

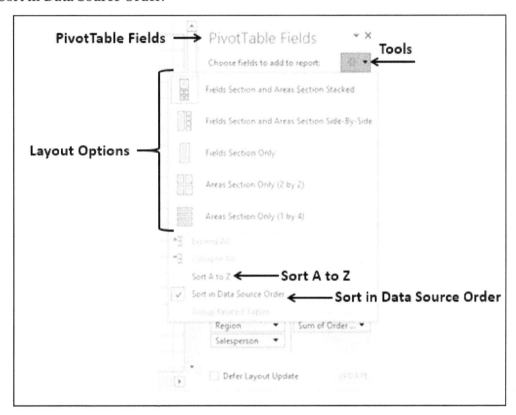

As you can observe in the above Fields list, the Sort order is by default – i.e. in Data Source Order. This means it is the order in which the columns in your data table appear. Normally, you can retain the default order. However, at times, you might encounter many fields in a table and might not be acquainted with them. In such a case, you can sort the fields in alphabetical order by clicking on – Sort A to Z in the dropdown list of Tools. Then, the PivotTable Fields list looks as follows:

Excel Pivot Tables - Areas

PivotTable areas are a part of PivotTable Fields Task Pane. By arranging the selected fields in the areas, you can arrive at different PivotTable layouts. As you can simply drag the fields across areas, you can quickly switch across the different layouts, summarizing the data, in a way you want.

There are four PivotTable areas available:

- ROWS.
- COLUMNS.
- FILTERS.
- $\sum$ VALUES (Read as Summarizing Values).

The message - Drag fields between areas below appear above the areas. With PivotTable Areas, you can choose:

- What fields to display as rows (ROWS area).
- What fields to display as columns (COLUMNS area).
- How to summarize your data ($\sum$ VALUES area).
- Filters for any of the fields (FILTERS area).

You can just drag the fields across these areas and observe how the PivotTable Layout changes.

ROWS

If you select the fields in the PivotTable Fields lists by just checking the boxes, all the non-numeric fields will automatically be added to the ROWS area, in the order you select. You can optionally, drag a field to the ROWS area. The fields that are put in the ROWS area appear as rows in the PivotTable, with the Row Labels being the values of the selected fields.

For example, consider the Sales data table.

- Drag the field Salesperson to the ROWS area.
- Drag the field Month to the ROWS area.

Your PivotTable appears with one column containing the Row Labels – Salesperson and Month and the last row as Grand Total.

COLUMNS

You can drag fields to the COLUMNS area.

The fields that are put in the COLUMNS area appear as columns in the PivotTable, with the Column Labels being the values of the selected fields.

Drag the field Region to the COLUMNS area. Your PivotTable appears with the first column containing the Row Labels, Salesperson and Month the next four columns containing the Column Labels – Region and the last column Grand Total as given below.

- Drag the field Month from ROWS to COLUMNS.
- Drag the field Region from COLUMNS to ROWS.

You can see that there are only five columns now – the first column with Row Labels, three columns with Column Labels, and the last column with Grand Total. The number of Rows and Columns is based on the number of values you have in those fields.

$\sum$ VALUES

The primary use of a PivotTable is to summarize values. Hence, by placing the fields by which you want to summarize the data in $\sum$ the VALUES area, you arrive at the summary table.

Drag the field Order Amount to $\sum$ VALUES.

Drag the field Region to above the field Salesperson in the ROWS area. This step is to change the nesting order. As you can observe, the data is summarized region-wise, salesperson-wise, and months. You have subtotals for each region, month-wise. You also have grand totals month-wise in the Grand Total row grand totals region-wise in the Grand Total column.

FILTERS

The Filters area is to place filters in PivotTable. Suppose you want to display results separately for the selected regions only.

Drag the field Region from the ROWS area to the FILTERS area. The filter Region will be placed above the Pivot Table. In case you do not have empty rows above the PivotTable, the PivotTable is pushed down inserting rows above the PivotTable for the filter.

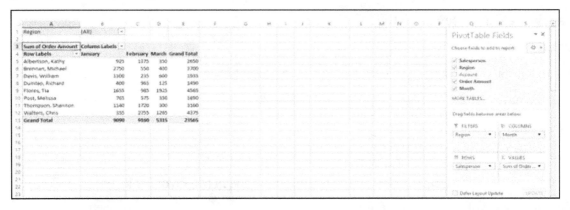

As you can observe, (ALL) appears in the filter by default, and the PivotTable displays data for all the values of the Region.

- Click on the arrow to the right of the filter.
- Check the box – Select Multiple Items.

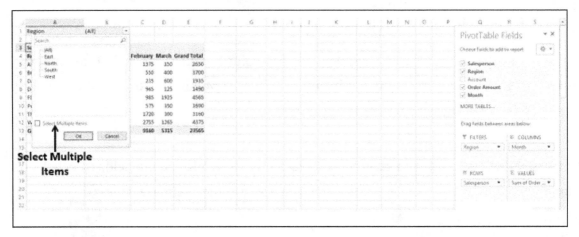

- Checkboxes will appear for all the options in the dropdown list. By default, all the boxes are checked.
- Check the boxes – North and South.
- Clear the other boxes. Click OK.

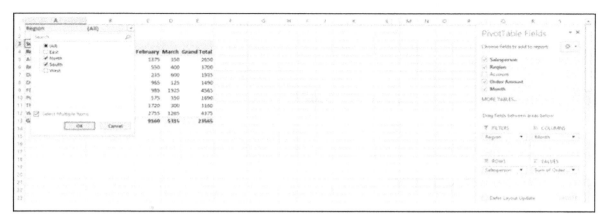

The PivotTable gets changed to reflect the filtered data.

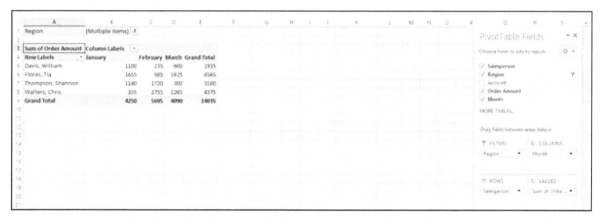

You can observe that the filter displays (Multiple Items). Therefore, when someone is looking at the Pivot Table, it is not immediately obvious what values are filtered.

Excel Pivot Tables - Exploring Data

Excel PivotTable allows you to explore and extract significant data from an Excel table or a range of data. There are several ways of doing this and you can choose the ones that are best suited to your data. Further, while you are exploring the data, you can view the different combinations instantly as you change your choices to pick the data values. You can do the following with a PivotTable:

- Sort the data.
- Filter the data.
- Nest the PivotTable fields.
- Expand and Collapse the fields.
- Group and ungroup field values.
- Sorting and Filtering Data

You can sort the data in a PivotTable in ascending or descending order of the field values. You can also sort by subtotals from largest to smallest or smallest to largest values. You can also set sort options.

Nesting, Expanding, And Collapsing Fields

You can nest fields in a PivotTable to show a hierarchy, if relevant to your data. When you have nested fields in your PivotTable, you can expand and collapse the values of those fields.

Excel Pivot Tables - Sorting Data

You can sort the data in a PivotTable so that it will be easy for you to find the items you want to analyze. You can sort the data from lowest to highest values or highest to lowest values or in any other custom order that you choose. Consider the following PivotTable wherein you have the summarized sales data region-wise, salesperson-wise, and month-wise.

	A	B	C	D	E
1					
2					
3	Sum of Order Amount	Column Labels ▾			
4	Row Labels ▾	January	February	March	Grand Total
5	⊟East	1690	1950	700	4340
6	Albertson, Kathy	925	1375	350	2650
7	Post, Melissa	765	575	350	1690
8	⊟North	1140	1720	300	3160
9	Thompson, Shannon	1140	1720	300	3160 ← PivotTable
10	⊟South	3110	3975	3790	10875
11	Davis, William	1100	235	600	1935
12	Flores, Tia	1655	985	1925	4565
13	Walters, Chris	355	2755	1265	4375
14	⊟West	3150	1515	525	5190
15	Brennan, Michael	2750	550	400	3700
16	Dumlao, Richard	400	965	125	1490
17	Grand Total	9090	9160	5315	23565

Sorting On Fields

You can sort the data in the above PivotTable on Fields that are in Rows or Columns – Region, Salesperson, and Month. To sort the PivotTable with the field Salesperson, proceed as follows:

- Click the arrow Down Arrow in the Row Labels.
- Select Salesperson in the Select Field box from the dropdown list.

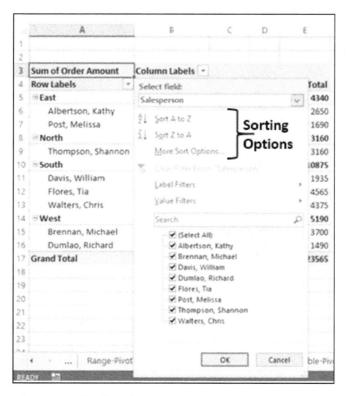

The following sorting options are displayed:

- Sort A to Z.

- Sort Z to A.

- More Sort Options.

Further, the Salesperson field is sorted in ascending order, by default. Click Sort Z to A.

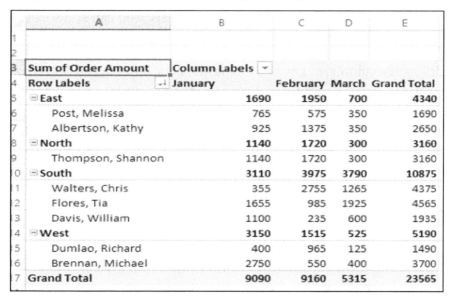

Sum of Order Amount	Column Labels			
Row Labels	January	February	March	Grand Total
East	1690	1950	700	4340
Post, Melissa	765	575	350	1690
Albertson, Kathy	925	1375	350	2650
North	1140	1720	300	3160
Thompson, Shannon	1140	1720	300	3160
South	3110	3975	3790	10875
Walters, Chris	355	2755	1265	4375
Flores, Tia	1655	985	1925	4565
Davis, William	1100	235	600	1935
West	3150	1515	525	5190
Dumlao, Richard	400	965	125	1490
Brennan, Michael	2750	550	400	3700
Grand Total	9090	9160	5315	23565

The Salesperson field will be sorted in descending order. In the same way, you can sort the field in the column, Month, by clicking on the arrow Down Arrow in the column labels.

Sorting On Subtotals

Suppose you want to sort the PivotTable based on total order amount – highest to lowest in every Region. That is, you want to sort the PivotTable on subtotals.

Row Labels	January	February	March	Grand Total	
⊟ East	1690	1950	700	4340	
Albertson, Kathy	925	1375	350	2650	Subtotals
Post, Melissa	765	575	350	1690	
⊟ North	1140	1720	300	3160	
Thompson, Shannon	1140	1720	300	3160	
⊟ South	3110	3975	3790	10875	
Davis, William	1100	235	600	1935	
Flores, Tia	1655	985	1925	4565	
Walters, Chris	355	2755	1265	4375	
⊟ West	3150	1515	525	5190	
Brennan, Michael	2750	550	400	3700	
Dumlao, Richard	400	965	125	1490	
Grand Total	9090	9160	5315	23565	

(Sum of Order Amount — Column Labels)

You can see that there is no arrow Down Arrow for subtotals. You can still sort the PivotTable on subtotals as follows:

- Right-click on the subtotal of any of the Salespersons in the Grand Total column.
- Select Sort from the dropdown list.
- Another dropdown list appears with the sorting options – Sort Smallest to Largest, Sort Largest to Smallest, and More Sort Options. Select Sort Largest to Smallest.

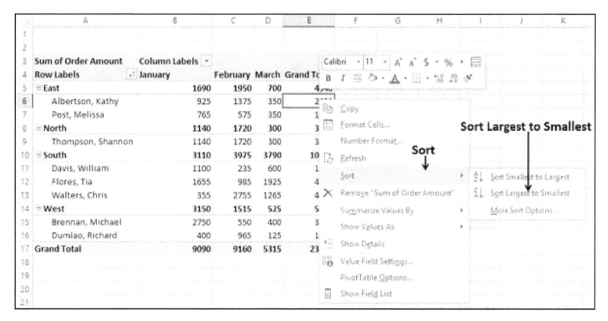

The subtotals in the Grand Total column are sorted from highest to lowest values, in every region.

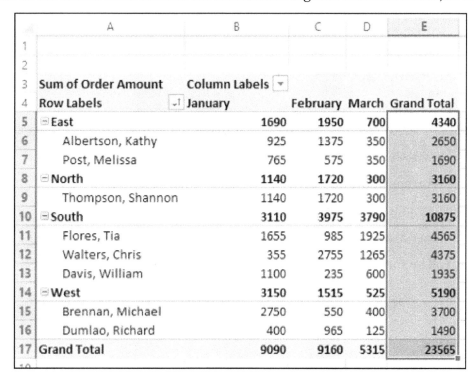

Likewise, if you want to sort the PivotTable on subtotals region-wise, do the following:

- Right-click on the subtotal of any of the regions in the Grand Total column.
- Click Sort in the dropdown list.

- Click Sort Largest to Smallest in the second dropdown list. The PivotTable will get sorted on subtotals region-wise.

	A	B	C	D	E
1					
2					
3	Sum of Order Amount	Column Labels ▾			
4	Row Labels ↓	January	February	March	Grand Total
5	⊟ South	3110	3975	3790	10875
6	Davis, William	1100	235	600	1935
7	Flores, Tia	1655	985	1925	4565
8	Walters, Chris	355	2755	1265	4375
9	⊟ West	3150	1515	525	5190
10	Brennan, Michael	2750	550	400	3700
11	Dumlao, Richard	400	965	125	1490
12	⊟ East	1690	1950	700	4340
13	Albertson, Kathy	925	1375	350	2650
14	Post, Melissa	765	575	350	1690
15	⊟ North	1140	1720	300	3160
16	Thompson, Shannon	1140	1720	300	3160
17	Grand Total	9090	9160	5315	23565

As you can observe, South has the highest order amount while North has the lowest. You can also sort the PivotTable based on the total amount month wise as follows:

- Right-click on any of the Subtotals in the Grand Total row.
- Select Sort from the dropdown list.
- Select Sort Largest to Smallest from the second dropdown list.

The PivotTable will be sorted on the total amount month-wise.

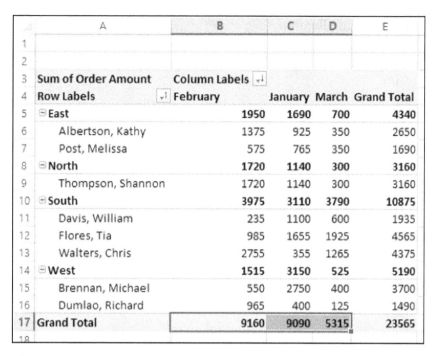

Sum of Order Amount	Column Labels			
Row Labels	February	January	March	Grand Total
⊟ East	1950	1690	700	4340
Albertson, Kathy	1375	925	350	2650
Post, Melissa	575	765	350	1690
⊟ North	1720	1140	300	3160
Thompson, Shannon	1720	1140	300	3160
⊟ South	3975	3110	3790	10875
Davis, William	235	1100	600	1935
Flores, Tia	985	1655	1925	4565
Walters, Chris	2755	355	1265	4375
⊟ West	1515	3150	525	5190
Brennan, Michael	550	2750	400	3700
Dumlao, Richard	965	400	125	1490
Grand Total	9160	9090	5315	23565

You can observe that February has the highest order amount while March has the lowest.

More Sort Options

Suppose you want to sort the PivotTable on the total amount region-wise in January.

- Click on the arrow Down Arrow in Row Labels.
- Select More Sort Options from the dropdown list. The Sort (Region) dialog box appears.

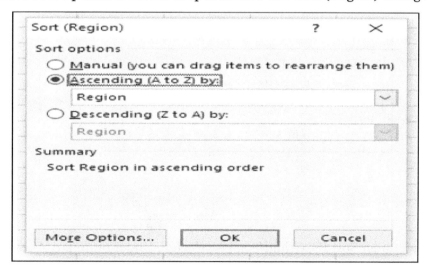

As you can observe, under Summary, the current Sort order is given as Sort Region in ascending order. Ascending (A to Z) is selected under Sort Options. In the box below that, Region is displayed.

- Click the box containing Region.
- Click Sum of Order Amount.

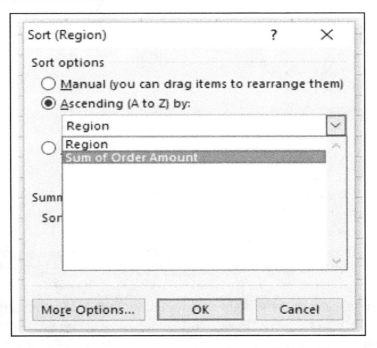

Click the More Options button. The More Sort Options (Region) dialog box appears.

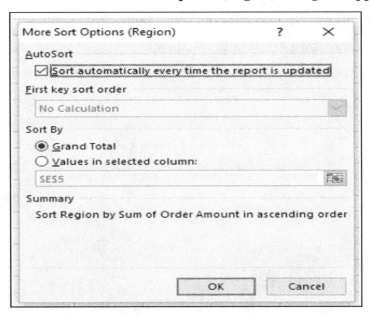

As you can observe, under Sort By, Grand Total is selected. Under Summary, the current sort order is given as Sort Region by Sum of Order Amount in ascending order.

- Click Values in the selected column: under Sort By.

- In the box below that, type B5.

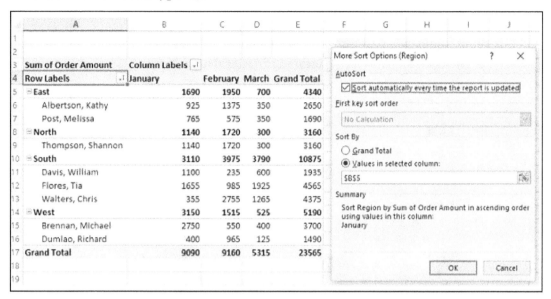

- As you can observe, under Summary, the current sort order is given as follows:
- Sort Region by Sum of Order Amount in ascending order using values in this column: January. Click OK.
- The Sort (Region) dialog box appears. Select Descending (Z to A) by: under Sort Options.

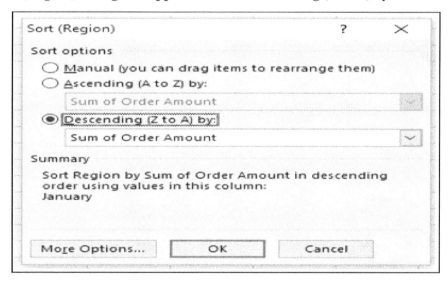

Under Summary, the current sort order is given as follows:

Sort Region by Sum of Order Amount in descending order, using values in this column: January. Click OK. The PivotTable will be sorted on region, using values in January.

	A	B	C	D	E
1					
2					
3	Sum of Order Amount	Column Labels ⌄			
4	Row Labels ⌄	January	February	March	Grand Total
5	⊟West	3150	1515	525	5190
6	Brennan, Michael	2750	550	400	3700
7	Dumlao, Richard	400	965	125	1490
8	⊟South	3110	3975	3790	10875
9	Davis, William	1100	235	600	1935
10	Flores, Tia	1655	985	1925	4565
11	Walters, Chris	355	2755	1265	4375
12	⊟East	1690	1950	700	4340
13	Albertson, Kathy	925	1375	350	2650
14	Post, Melissa	765	575	350	1690
15	⊟North	1140	1720	300	3160
16	Thompson, Shannon	1140	1720	300	3160
17	Grand Total	9090	9160	5315	23565

As you can observe, in January, West has the highest order amount while North has the lowest.

Sorting Data Manually

In the PivotTable, the data is sorted automatically by the sorting option that you have chosen. This is termed as AutoSort. Place the cursor on the arrow Down Arrow in Row Labels or Column Labels.

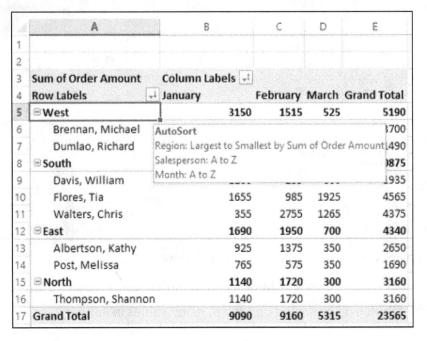

AutoSort appears, showing the current sort order for each of the fields in the PivotTable. Now, suppose you want to sort the field Region in order – East, West, North, and South. You can do this manually, as follows:

- Click the arrow Down Arrow in Row Labels.
- Select Region in the Select Field box from the dropdown list.
- Click More Sort Options. The Sort (Region) dialog box appears.
- Select Manual (you can drag items to rearrange them).
- Click OK.

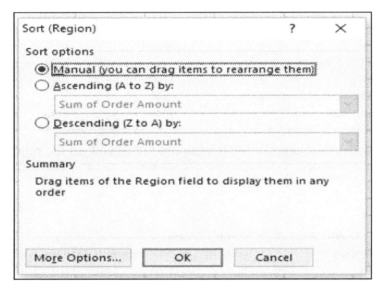

Under Summary, the current sort order is given as Drag items of the Region field to display them in any order. Click on the East and drag it to the top. While you are dragging East, a horizontal green bar appears across the entire row moves.

	A	B	C	D	E
3	Sum of Order Amount	Column Labels ⌄			
4	Row Labels ⌄	January	February	March	Grand Total
5	⊟West	3150	1515	525	5190
6	Brennan, Michael	2750	550	400	3700
7	Dumlao, Richard	400	965	125	1490
8	⊟South	3110	3975	3790	10875
9	Davis, William (A8:E8)	1100	235	600	1935
10	Flores, Tia	1655	985	1925	4565
11	Walters, Chris	355	2755	1265	4375
12	⊟East	1690	1950	700	4340
13	Albertson, Kathy	925	1375	350	2650
14	Post, Melissa	765	575	350	1690
15	⊟North	1140	1720	300	3160
16	Thompson, Shannon	1140	1720	300	3160
17	Grand Total	9090	9160	5315	23565

Repeat the dragging with other items of the Region field until you get the required arrangement.

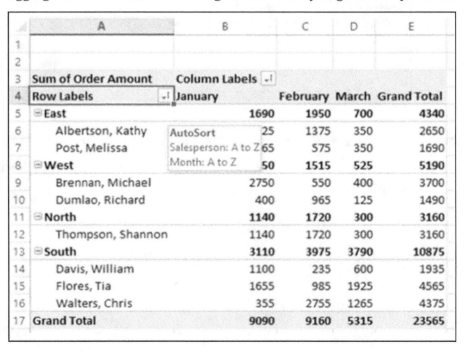

	A	B	C	D	E
3	Sum of Order Amount	Column Labels ⌄			
4	Row Labels ⌄	January	February	March	Grand Total
5	⊟East	1690	1950	700	4340
6	Albertson, Kathy	*AutoSort* 25	1375	350	2650
7	Post, Melissa	*Salesperson: A to Z* 65	575	350	1690
8	⊟West	*Month: A to Z* 50	1515	525	5190
9	Brennan, Michael	2750	550	400	3700
10	Dumlao, Richard	400	965	125	1490
11	⊟North	1140	1720	300	3160
12	Thompson, Shannon	1140	1720	300	3160
13	⊟South	3110	3975	3790	10875
14	Davis, William	1100	235	600	1935
15	Flores, Tia	1655	985	1925	4565
16	Walters, Chris	355	2755	1265	4375
17	Grand Total	9090	9160	5315	23565

You Can Observe The Following:

The items of the nested field – Salesperson also move along with the corresponding Region field item. Further, the values in the other columns also moved accordingly. If you place the cursor on the arrow Down Arrow in Row Labels or Column Labels, AutoSort appears showing the current sort order of the fields Salesperson and Month only. As you have sorted the Region field manually, it will not show up in AutoSort.

Note: You cannot use this manual dragging of items of the field that is in Σ the VALUES area of the PivotTable Fields list. Therefore, you cannot drag the Sum of Order Amount values in this Pivot Table.

Setting Sort Options

In the previous section, you have learned how to set the sorting option for a field to manual. You have some more sort options that you can set as follows:

- Click the arrow Down Arrow in Row Labels.
- Select Region in the Select Field box.
- Click More Sort Options. The Sort (Region) dialog box appears.
- Click the More Options button.

More Sort Options (Region) dialog box appears. You can set more sort options in this dialog box.

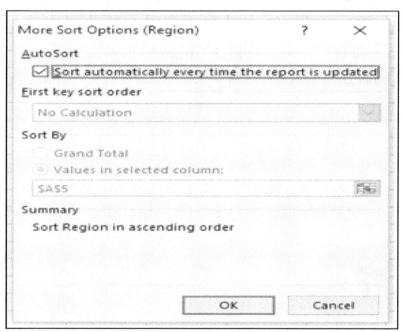

- Under AutoSort, you can check or uncheck the box - Sort automatically every time the report is updated, to allow or stop automatic sorting whenever the PivotTable data is updated.
- Uncheck the box – Sort automatically every time the report is updated.

- Now, the First key sort order option becomes available. You can use this option to select the custom order you want to use.
- Click the box under First key sort order.

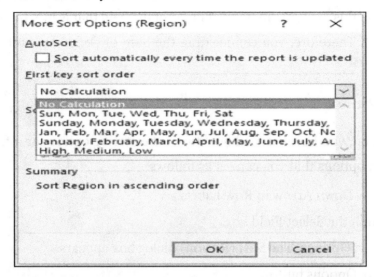

As you can observe, day-of-the-week and month-of-the-year custom lists are provided in the dropdown list. You can use any of these, or you can use your custom list such as High, Medium, Low, or the sizes list S, M, L, XL that are not in alphabetical order.

You can create your custom lists from the FILE tab on the Ribbon. FILE → Options. In the Excel Options dialog box, click on advanced and browse to General. You will find the Edit Custom Lists button next to Create lists for use in sort and fill sequences.

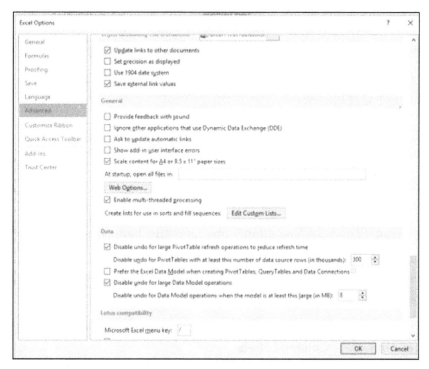

Note that a custom list sort order is not retained when you update (refresh) data in your PivotTable. Under Sort By, you can click Grand Total or Values in selected columns to sort by these values. This option is not available when you set sorting to Manual.

Points To Consider While Sorting Pivottables

When you sort data in a PivotTable, remember the following:

- Data that has leading spaces will affect the sort results. Remove any leading spaces before you sort the data.
- You cannot sort case-sensitive text entries.
- You cannot sort data by a specific format such as cell or font color.
- You cannot sort data by conditional formatting indicators, such as icon sets.

Excel Pivot Tables - Filtering Data

You might have to do an in-depth analysis on a subset of your PivotTable data. This might be because you have large data and your focus is required on a smaller portion of the data or irrespective of the size of the data, your focus is required on certain specific data. You can filter the data in the PivotTable based on a subset of the values of one or more fields. There are several ways to do that as follows:

- Filtering using Slicers.
- Filtering using Report Filters.
- Filtering data manually.
- Filtering using Label Filters.
- Filtering using Value Filters.
- Filtering using Date Filters.
- Filtering using Top 10 Filter.
- Filtering using Timeline.

Consider the following PivotTable wherein you have the summarized sales data region-wise, salesperson wise and month-wise.

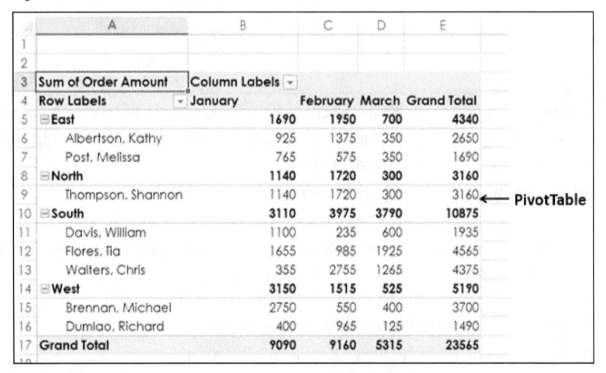

Sum of Order Amount	Column Labels			
Row Labels	January	February	March	Grand Total
⊟East	1690	1950	700	4340
Albertson, Kathy	925	1375	350	2650
Post, Melissa	765	575	350	1690
⊟North	1140	1720	300	3160
Thompson, Shannon	1140	1720	300	3160
⊟South	3110	3975	3790	10875
Davis, William	1100	235	600	1935
Flores, Tia	1655	985	1925	4565
Walters, Chris	355	2755	1265	4375
⊟West	3150	1515	525	5190
Brennan, Michael	2750	550	400	3700
Dumlao, Richard	400	965	125	1490
Grand Total	9090	9160	5315	23565

← PivotTable

Report Filters

You can assign a Filter to one of the fields so that you can dynamically change the PivotTable based on the values of that field. Drag Region from Rows to Filters in the PivotTable Areas.

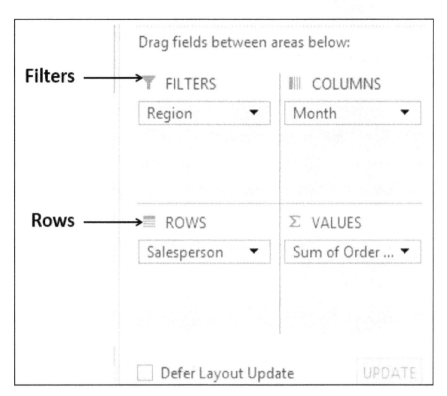

The Filter with the label as Region appears above the PivotTable (in case you do not have empty rows above your PivotTable, PivotTable gets pushed down to make space for the Filter.

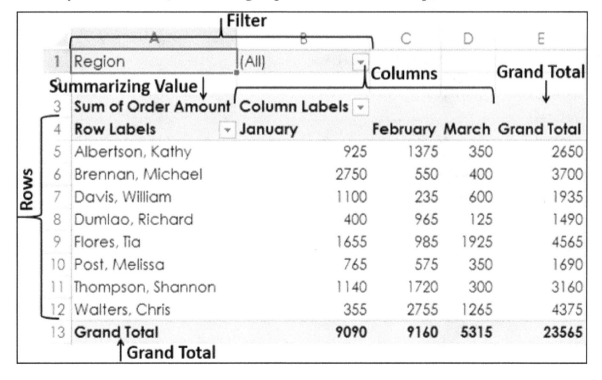

You Will Observe That

- Salesperson values appear in rows.

- Month values appear in columns.

- Region Filter appears on the top with default selected as ALL.

- Summarizing value is Sum of Order Amount.

- Sum of Order Amount Salesperson-wise appears in the Column Grand Total.

- Sum of Order Amount Month-wise appears in the row Grand Total.

- Click on the arrow in the box to the right of the Filter Region.

A drop-down list with the values of the field Region appears. Check the box Select Multiple Items.

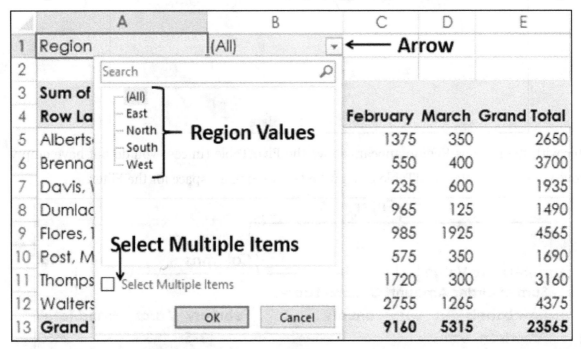

By default, all the boxes are checked. Uncheck the box (All). All the boxes will be unchecked.

Then check the boxes - South and West and click OK.

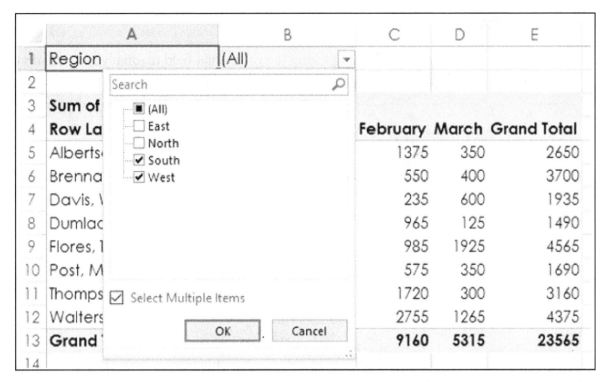

The data about the South and West regions only will get summarized.

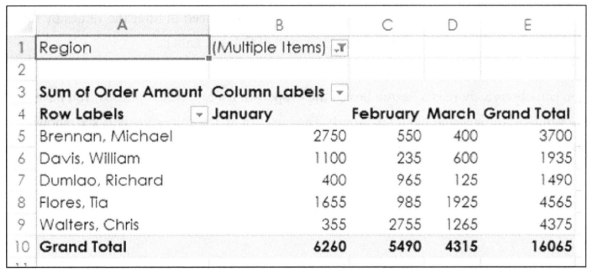

In the cell next to the Filter Region - (Multiple Items) is displayed, indicating that you have selected more than one item. However, how many items and/or which items are not known from the report that is displayed. In such a case, using Slicers is a better option for filtering.

Manual Filtering

- You can also filter the PivotTable by picking the values of a field manually. You can do this by clicking on the arrow in the Row Labels or Column Labels cell.

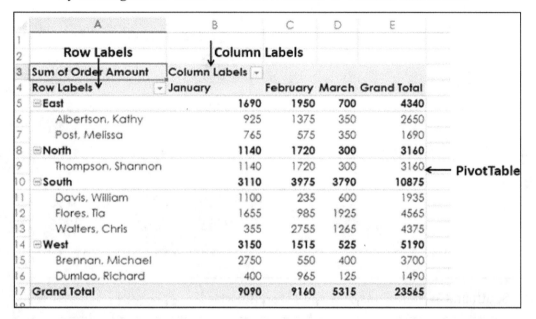

- Suppose you want to analyze only February data. You need to filter the values by the field Month. As you can observe, the Month is part of Column Labels.
- Click on the arrow in the Column Labels cell.

As you can observe, there is a Search box in the dropdown list and below the box, you have the list of the values of the selected field, i.e. Month. The boxes of all the values are checked, showing that all the values of that field are selected.

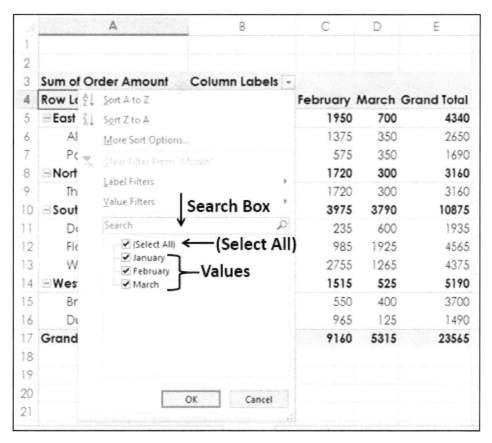

- Uncheck the (Select All) box at the top of the list of values.
- Check the boxes of the values you want to show in your PivotTable, in this case, February, and click OK.

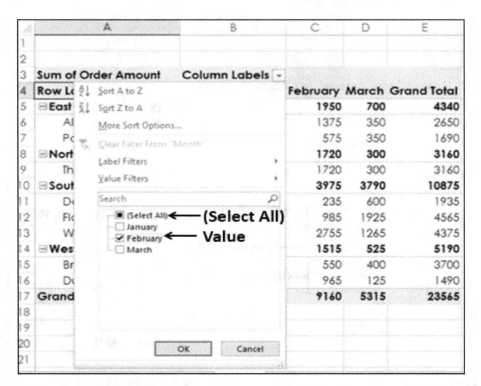

The PivotTable displays only those values that are related to the selected Month field value – February. You can observe that the filtering arrow changes to the icon to indicate that a filter is applied. Place the cursor on the icon.

Sum of Order Amount	Column Labels	
Row Labels	February	Grand Total
⊟East	195⟨	50
Albertson, Kathy	137ʊ	⟋ʊ75
Post, Melissa	575	575
⊟North	1720	1720
Thompson, Shannon	1720	1720
⊟South	3975	3975
Davis, William	235	235
Flores, Tia	985	985
Walters, Chris	2755	2755
⊟West	1515	1515
Brennan, Michael	550	550
Dumlao, Richard	965	965
Grand Total	9160	9160

You can observe that is displayed indicating that the Manual Filter is applied on the field- Month. If you want to change the filter selection value, do the following:

- Click the icon.
- Check / uncheck the boxes of the values.

If all the values of the field are not visible in the list, drag the handle in the bottom-right corner of the dropdown to enlarge it. Alternatively, if you know the value, type it in the Search box.

Suppose you want to apply another filter on the above filtered PivotTable. For example, you want to display the data of that of Walters, Chris for February. You need to refine your filtering by adding another filter for the field Salesperson. As you can observe, Salesperson is part of Row Labels.

- Click on the arrow in the Row Labels cell.

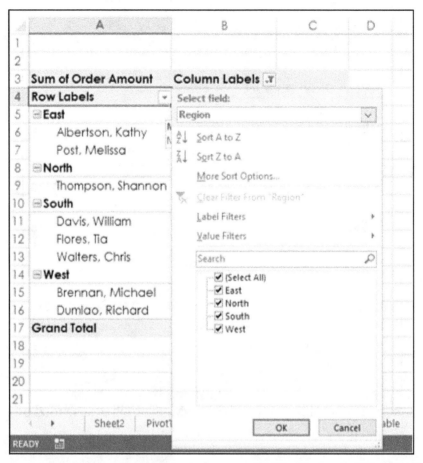

The list of the values of the field – Region is displayed. This is because Region is at the outer level of Salesperson in the nesting order. You also have an additional option – Select Field. Click on the Select Field box.

- Click Salesperson from the dropdown list. The list of the values of the field – Salesperson will be displayed.
- Uncheck (Select All) and check Walters, Chris.
- Click OK.

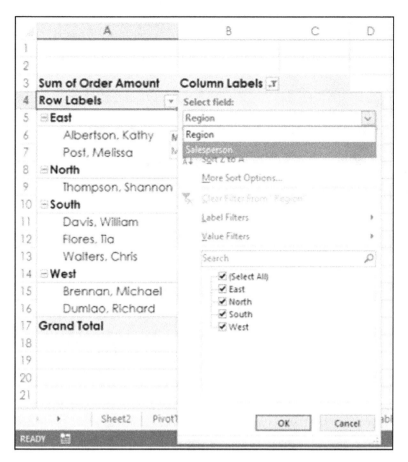

The PivotTable displays only those values that are related to the selected Month field value – February and Salesperson field value - Walters, Chris.

The filtering arrow for Row Labels also changes to the icon to indicate that a filter is applied. Place the cursor on the icon on either Row Labels or Column Labels.

	A	B	C
1			
2			
3	Sum of Order Amount	Column Labels ⏷	
4	Row Labels ⏷	February	Grand Total
5	⊟South	275.	Manual Filters 55
6	Walters, Chris	275.	Salesperson 55
7	Grand Total	2755	Month 2755

A text box is displayed indicating that the Manual Filter is applied on the fields – Month, and Salesperson.

You can thus filter the PivotTable manually based on any number of fields and any number of values.

Filtering By Text

If you have fields that contain text, you can filter the PivotTable by Text, provided the corresponding field label is text-based. For example, consider the following Employee data.

	A	B	C	D	E	F	G	H
1								
2		EmployeeID ⏷	ManagerLevel ⏷	Title ⏷	BirthDate ⏷	MaritalStatus ⏷	Gender ⏷	HireDate ⏷
3		1	0	Chief Executive Officer	1/29/1969	S	M	1/14/2014
4		2	1	Vice President of Engineering	8/1/1971	S	F	1/31/2013
5		3	2	Engineering Manager	11/12/1974	M	M	11/11/2013
6		4	3	Senior Tool Designer	12/23/1974	S	M	12/5/2013
7		5	3	Design Engineer	9/27/1952	M	F	1/6/2013
8		6	3	Design Engineer	3/11/1959	M	M	1/24/2013
9		7	3	Research and Development Manager	2/24/1987	M	M	2/8/2014
10		8	4	Research and Development Engineer	6/5/1986	S	F	12/29/2013
11		9	4	Research and Development Engineer	1/21/1979	M	F	1/16/2014
12		10	4	Research and Development Manager	11/30/1984	M	M	5/3/2014
13		11	3	Senior Tool Designer	1/17/1978	S	M	12/5/2015
14		12	4	Tool Designer	7/29/1959	M	M	12/11/2013
15		13	4	Tool Designer	5/28/1989	M	F	12/23/2015
16		14	3	Senior Design Engineer	6/16/1979	S	M	12/30/2015
17		15	3	Design Engineer	5/2/1961	M	F	1/18/2014
18		16	1	Marketing Manager	3/19/1975	S	M	12/20/2013
19		17	2	Marketing Assistant	5/3/1987	S	M	1/26/2013
20		18	2	Marketing Specialist	3/6/1978	S	M	2/7/2014
21		19	2	Marketing Assistant	1/29/1978	S	F	2/14/2014
22		20	2	Marketing Assistant	3/17/1975	M	F	1/7/2014
23		21	2	Marketing Specialist	2/4/1986	M	M	3/2/2014

The data has the details of the employees – EmployeeID, Title, BirthDate, marital status, Gender, and HireDate. Additionally, the data also has the manager level of the employee (levels 0 – 4).

Suppose you have to do some analysis on the number of employees reporting to a given employee by title. You can create a pivotTable as given below.

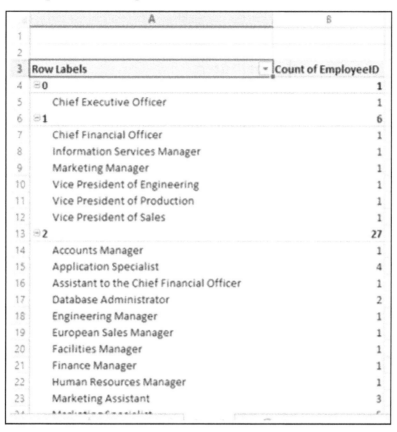

You might want to know how many employees with 'Manager' in their title have employees reporting to them. As the Label Title is text-based, you can apply the Label Filter on the Title field as follows:

- Click on the arrow in the Row Labels cell.
- Select Title in the Select Field box from the drop-down list.
- Click on Label Filters.
- Click on Contains in the second dropdown list.

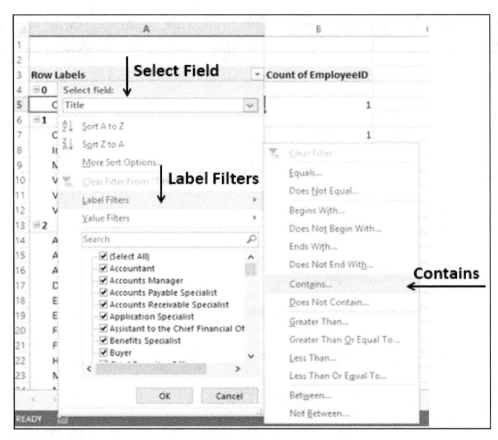

The label Filter (Title) dialog box appears. Type Manager in the box next to Contains. Click OK.

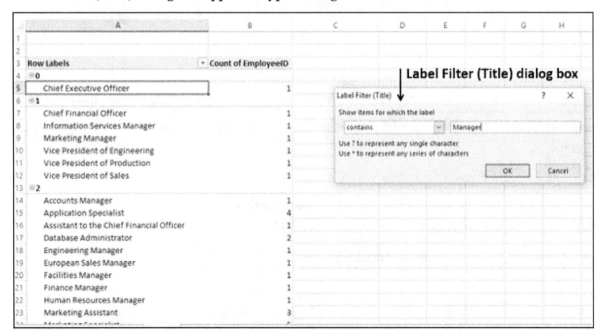

The PivotTable will be filtered to the Title values containing 'Manager'.

- Click the icon.

You can see that is displayed indicating the following:

- The Label Filter is applied on the field – Title, and
- What the applied Label Filter is.

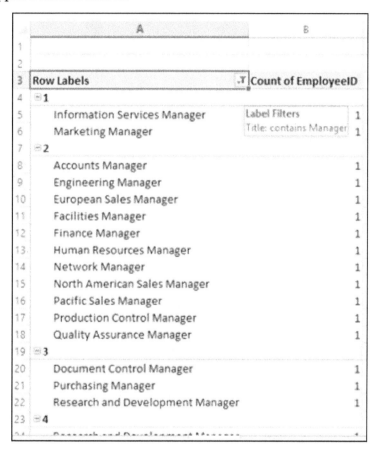

Filtering By Values

You might want to know the titles of the employees who have more than 25 employees reporting to them. For this, you can apply the Value Filter on the Title field as follows:

- Click on the arrow in the Row Labels cell.
- Select Title in the Select Field box from the drop-down list.
- Click on Value Filters.
- Select Greater than or equal to from the second dropdown list.

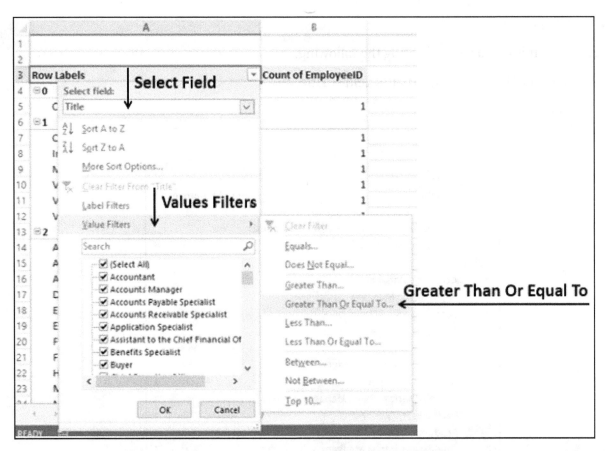

The Value Filter (Title) dialog box appears. Type 25 in the right side box. The PivotTable will be filtered to display the employee titles who have more than 25 employees reporting to them.

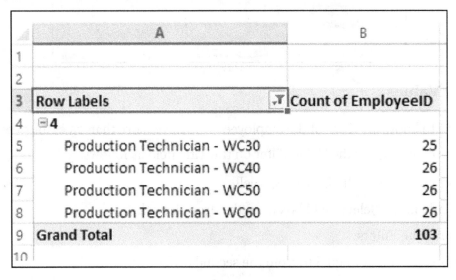

Filtering By Dates

You might want to display the data of all the employees who were hired in the fiscal year 2015-15. You can use Data Filters for the same as follows:

- Include the HireDate field in the PivotTable. Now, you do not require manager data and so remove the ManagerLevel field from the PivotTable.

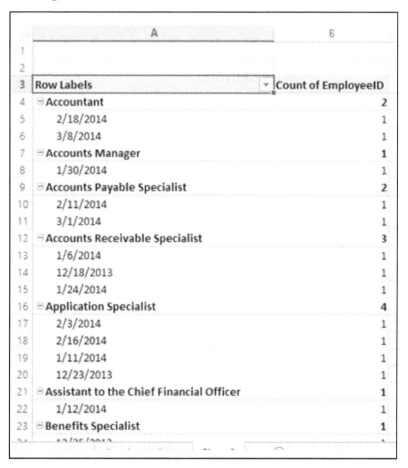

Now that you have a Date field in the PivotTable, you can use Date Filters.

- Click the arrow in the Row Labels cell.
- Select HireDate in the Select Field box from the drop-down list.
- Click Date Filters.
- Select Between from the second dropdown list.

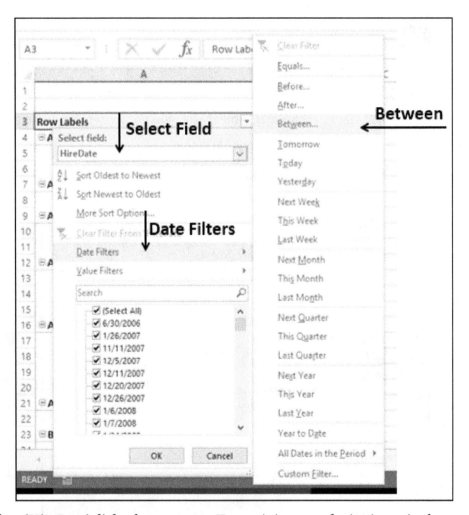

The Date Filter (HireDate) dialog box appears. Type 4/1/2014 and 3/31/2015 in the two Date boxes. Click OK.

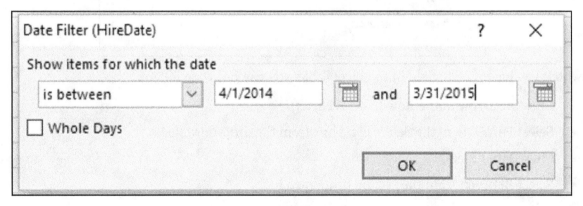

The PivotTable will be filtered to display only the data with HireDate between 1st April 2014 and 31st March 2015.

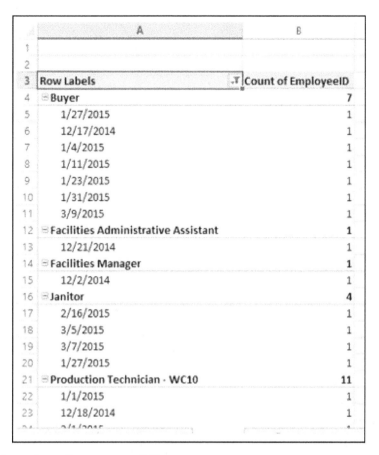

Row Labels	Count of EmployeeID
⊟ Buyer	7
1/27/2015	1
12/17/2014	1
1/4/2015	1
1/11/2015	1
1/23/2015	1
1/31/2015	1
3/9/2015	1
⊟ Facilities Administrative Assistant	1
12/21/2014	1
⊟ Facilities Manager	1
12/2/2014	1
⊟ Janitor	4
2/16/2015	1
3/5/2015	1
3/7/2015	1
1/27/2015	1
⊟ Production Technician - WC10	11
1/1/2015	1
12/18/2014	1

You can group the dates into Quarters as follows:

- Right-click on any of the dates. The Grouping dialog box appears.
- Type 4/1/2014 in the box Starting at. Check the box.
- Type 3/31/2015 in the box Ending at. Check the box.
- Click Quarters in the box under By.

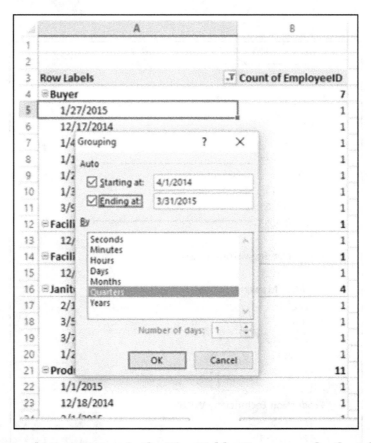

The dates will be grouped into quarters in the PivotTable. You can make the table look compact by dragging the field HireDate from the ROWS area to the COLUMNS area.

You will be able to know how many employees were hired during the fiscal year, quarter-wise.

Count of EmployeeID	Column Labels				
Row Labels	Qtr1	Qtr2	Qtr3	Qtr4	Grand Total
Accountant	2				2
Accounts Manager	1				1
Accounts Payable Specialist	2				2
Accounts Receivable Specialist	2			1	3
Application Specialist	3			1	4
Assistant to the Chief Financial Officer	1				1
Benefits Specialist				1	1
Buyer	8			1	9
Chief Executive Officer	1				1
Chief Financial Officer	1				1
Control Specialist	1			1	2
Database Administrator	2				2
Design Engineer	3				3
Document Control Assistant	2				2
Document Control Manager	1				1
Engineering Manager				1	1
European Sales Manager			1		1
Facilities Administrative Assistant				1	1
Facilities Manager				1	1

Filtering Using Top 10 Filter

You can use the Top 10 Filter to display the top few or bottom few values of a field in the PivotTable.

- Click the arrow in the Row Labels cell.
- Click Value Filters.
- Click Top 10 in the second dropdown list.

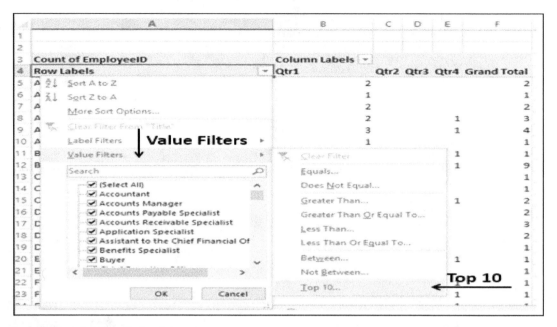

The top 10 Filter (Title) dialog box appears.

- In the first box, click on Top (You can choose Bottom also).

- In the second box, enter a number, say, 7.

- In the third box, you have three options by which you can filter.

- Click on Items to filter by several items.

- Click on Percent to filter by percentage.

- Click on Sum to filter by sum.

- As you have a count of EmployeeID, click Items.

- In the fourth box, click on the field Count of EmployeeID.

- Click OK.

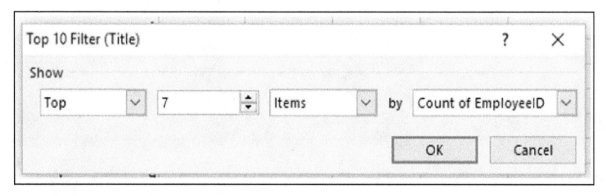

The top seven values by a count of EmployeeID will be displayed in the PivotTable. As you can observe, the highest number of hires in the fiscal year is that of Production Technicians and a predominant number of these are in Qtr1.

| Count of EmployeeID | Column Labels | | | | |
Row Labels	Qtr1	Qtr2	Qtr3	Qtr4	Grand Total
Production Technician - WC10	13			4	17
Production Technician - WC20	16			6	22
Production Technician - WC30	17			8	25
Production Technician - WC40	17			9	26
Production Technician - WC45	10			5	15
Production Technician - WC50	18			8	26
Production Technician - WC60	18	1		7	26
Grand Total	109	1		47	157

Filtering Using Timeline

If your PivotTable has a date field, you can filter the PivotTable using Timeline.

Create a PivotTable from the Employee Data that you used earlier and add the data to the Data Model in the Create PivotTable dialog box.

- Drag the field Title to the ROWS area.
- Drag the field EmployeeID to Σ the VALUES area and choose Count for calculation.

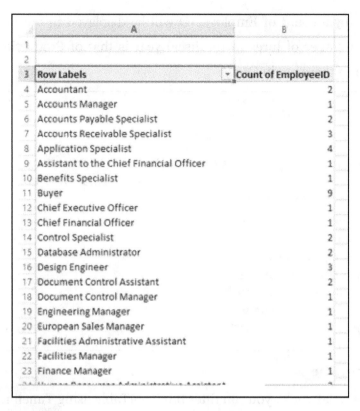

Row Labels	Count of EmployeeID
Accountant	2
Accounts Manager	1
Accounts Payable Specialist	2
Accounts Receivable Specialist	3
Application Specialist	4
Assistant to the Chief Financial Officer	1
Benefits Specialist	1
Buyer	9
Chief Executive Officer	1
Chief Financial Officer	1
Control Specialist	2
Database Administrator	2
Design Engineer	3
Document Control Assistant	2
Document Control Manager	1
Engineering Manager	1
European Sales Manager	1
Facilities Administrative Assistant	1
Facilities Manager	1
Finance Manager	1

- Click on the PivotTable.
- Click the INSERT tab.
- Click Timeline in the Filters group. The Insert Timelines dialog box appears.
- Check the box HireDate.

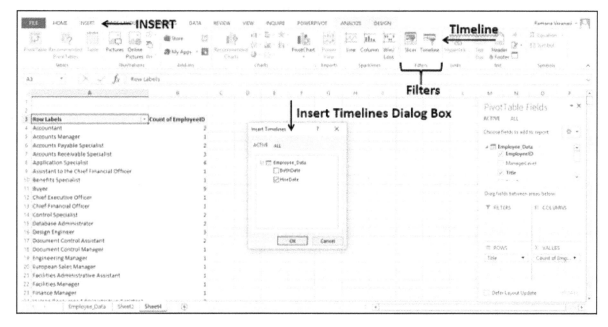

- Click OK. The Timeline appears in the worksheet.
- Timeline Tools appear on the Ribbon.

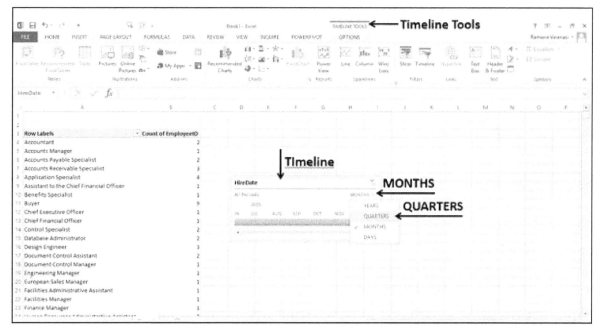

As you can observe, All Periods – in Months are displayed on the Timeline.

- Click on the arrow next to - MONTHS.
- Select QUARTERS from the drop-down list. The Timeline display changes to All Periods – in Quarters.

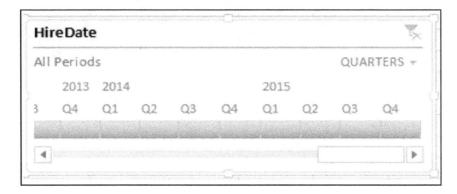

- Click on 2014 Q1.
- Keep the Shift key pressed and drag to 2014 Q4. The Timeline Period is selected for Q1 – Q4 2014.
- PivotTable is filtered to this Timeline Period.

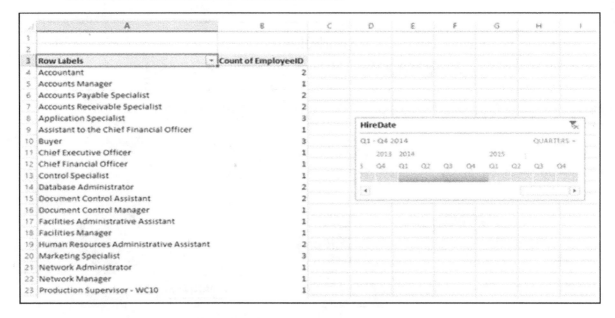

Clearing The Filters

You might have to clear the filters you have set from time to time to switch across different combinations and projections of your data. You can do this in several ways as follows:

Clearing All The Filters In A Pivottable

You can clear all the filters set in a PivotTable at one go as follows:

- Click the HOME tab on the Ribbon.
- Click Sort & Filter in the Editing group.

- Select Clear from the dropdown list.

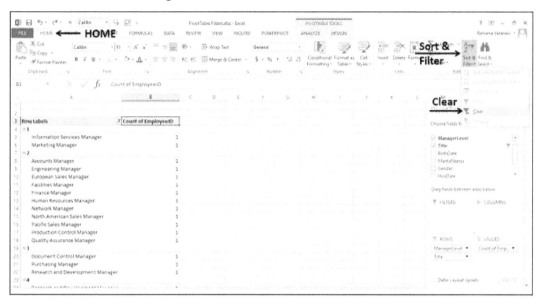

Clearing A Label, Date, Or Value Filter

To clear a Label, Date, or Value Filter do the following:

- Click on the icon in the Row Labels or Column Labels.
- Click on the   <field name> from which you want to clear the filter in the Select Field box in the dropdown list.
- Click on Clear Filter From <Filed Name> that appears in the dropdown list.
- Click OK. The specific filter will be cleared.

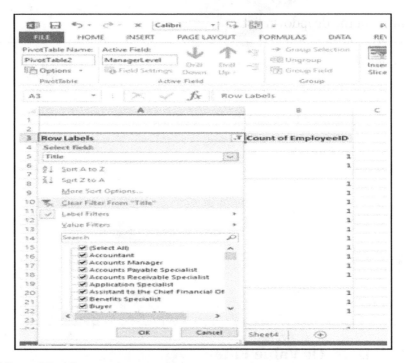

Excel Pivot Tables - Nesting

If you have more than one field in any of the PivotTable areas, then the PivotTable layout depends on the order you place the fields in that area. This is called the Nesting Order.

If you know how your data is structured, you can place the fields in the required order. If you are not sure about the structure of the data, you can change the order of the fields that instantly change the layout of the PivotTable.

Nesting Order Of The Fields

Consider the sales data example, where you have placed the fields in the following order:

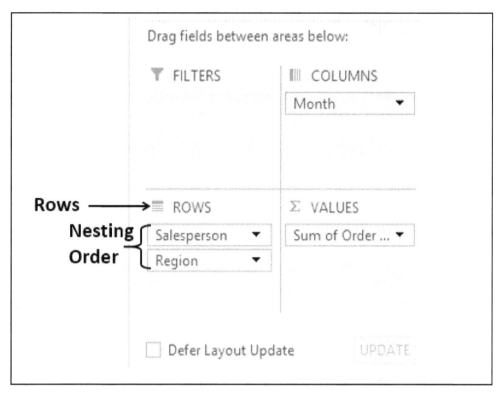

As you can see, in the rows area there are two fields – salesperson and region in that order. This order of the fields is called nesting order i.e. Salesperson first and Region next.

In the PivotTable, the values in the rows will be displayed based on this order.

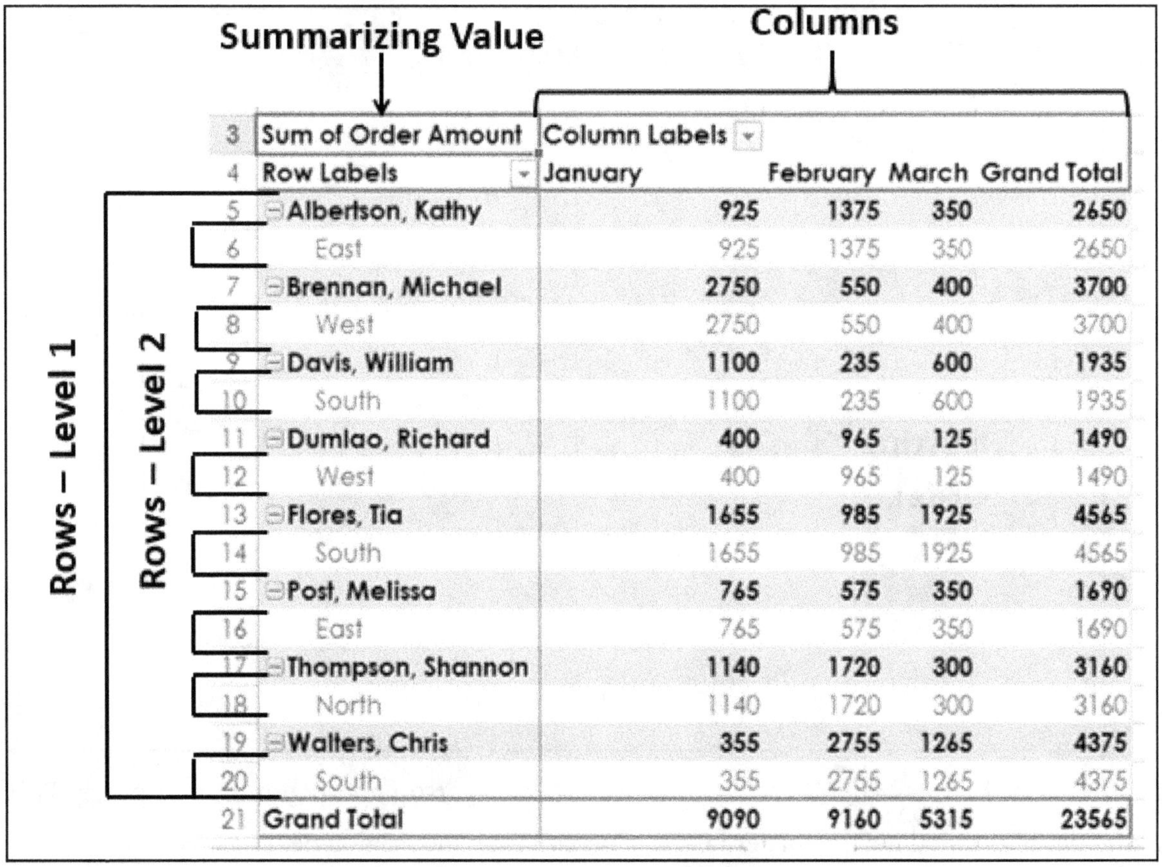

		Sum of Order Amount	Column Labels			
3		Sum of Order Amount	Column Labels			
4		Row Labels	January	February	March	Grand Total
5		Albertson, Kathy	925	1375	350	2650
6		East	925	1375	350	2650
7		Brennan, Michael	2750	550	400	3700
8		West	2750	550	400	3700
9		Davis, William	1100	235	600	1935
10		South	1100	235	600	1935
11		Dumlao, Richard	400	965	125	1490
12		West	400	965	125	1490
13		Flores, Tia	1655	985	1925	4565
14		South	1655	985	1925	4565
15		Post, Melissa	765	575	350	1690
16		East	765	575	350	1690
17		Thompson, Shannon	1140	1720	300	3160
18		North	1140	1720	300	3160
19		Walters, Chris	355	2755	1265	4375
20		South	355	2755	1265	4375
21		Grand Total	9090	9160	5315	23565

(Labels: Summarizing Value; Columns; Rows – Level 1; Rows – Level 2)

As you can observe, the values of the second field in the nesting order are embedded under each of the values of the first field.

In your data, each salesperson is associated with only one region, whereas most of the regions are associated with more than one salesperson. Hence, there is a possibility that if you reverse the nesting order, your PivotTable will look more meaningful.

Changing The Nesting Order

To change the nesting order of the fields in an area, just click the field and drag it to the position you want.

Click on the field Salesperson in the ROWS area, and drag it to below the field Region. Thus, you have changed the nesting order to, Region first and Salesperson next, as follows:

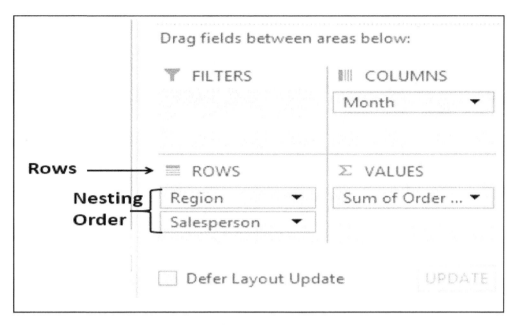

The resulting PivotTable will be as given below:

3	Sum of Order Amount	Column Labels			
4	Row Labels	January	February	March	Grand Total
5	⊟East	1690	1950	700	4340
6	Albertson, Kathy	925	1375	350	2650
7	Post, Melissa	765	575	350	1690
8	⊟North	1140	1720	300	3160
9	Thompson, Shannon	1140	1720	300	3160
10	⊟South	3110	3975	3790	10875
11	Davis, William	1100	235	600	1935
12	Flores, Tia	1655	985	1925	4565
13	Walters, Chris	355	2755	1265	4375
14	⊟West	3150	1515	525	5190
15	Brennan, Michael	2750	550	400	3700
16	Dumlao, Richard	400	965	125	1490
17	Grand Total	9090	9160	5315	23565

- You can observe that the Layout with the nesting order – Region and then Salesperson yields a better and compact report than the one with the nesting order – Salesperson and then Region.
- In case a Salesperson represents more than one area and you need to summarize the sales by Salesperson, then the previous Layout would have been a better option.

Excel Pivot Tables – Tools

In the worksheet containing a PivotTable, the Ribbon will contain the PivotTable Tools, with ANALYZE and DESIGN Tabs. The ANALYZE tab has several commands that will enable you to explore the data in the PivotTable. The DESIGN tab commands will be useful to structure the PivotTable with various report options and style options.

ANALYZE Commands

The commands on the Ribbon of ANALYZE tab include the following:

- Expanding and Collapsing a Field.
- Grouping and Ungrouping Field Values.
- Active Field Settings.
- PivotTable Options.

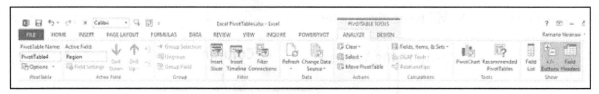

Expanding And Collapsing A Field

If you have nested fields in your PivotTable, you can expand and collapse a single item or you can expand and collapse all the items of the active field.

Consider the following PivotTable, wherein you have the Salesperson field nested under the Region field.

Sum of Order Amount	Column Labels ▼			
Row Labels ▼	January	February	March	Grand Total
⊟ East	1690	1950	700	4340
Albertson, Kathy	925	1375	350	2650
Post, Melissa	765	575	350	1690
⊟ North	1140	1720	300	3160
Thompson, Shannon	1140	1720	300	3160
⊟ South	3110	3975	3790	10875
Davis, William	1100	235	600	1935
Flores, Tia	1655	985	1925	4565
Walters, Chris	355	2755	1265	4375
⊟ West	3150	1515	525	5190
Brennan, Michael	2750	550	400	3700
Dumlao, Richard	400	965	125	1490
Grand Total	9090	9160	5315	23565

Click the symbol to the left of East. The item East of the field Region will collapse.

Sum of Order Amount	Column Labels ▼			
Row Labels ▼	January	February	March	Grand Total
⊞ East	1690	1950	700	4340
⊟ North	1140	1720	300	3160
Thompson, Shannon	1140	1720	300	3160
⊟ South	3110	3975	3790	10875
Davis, William	1100	235	600	1935
Flores, Tia	1655	985	1925	4565
Walters, Chris	355	2755	1265	4375
⊟ West	3150	1515	525	5190
Brennan, Michael	2750	550	400	3700
Dumlao, Richard	400	965	125	1490
Grand Total	9090	9160	5315	23565

As you can observe, the other items - North, South, and West of the field Region are not collapsed. If you want to collapse any of them, repeat the steps that you have done for East.

- Click on the symbol to the left of East. The item East of the field Region will expand.

If you want to collapse all the items of a field at once, do the following:

- Click any of the items of the field – Region.
- Click the ANALYZE tab on the Ribbon.
- Click Collapse Field in the Active Field group.

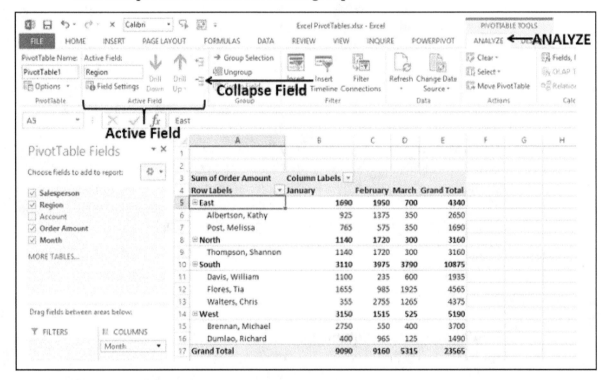

- All the items of the field Region will be collapsed.

	A	B	C	D	E
1					
2					
3	Sum of Order Amount	Column Labels ▾			
4	Row Labels ▾	January	February	March	Grand Total
5	⊞ East	1690	1950	700	4340
6	⊞ North	1140	1720	300	3160
7	⊞ South	3110	3975	3790	10875
8	⊞ West	3150	1515	525	5190
9	Grand Total	9090	9160	5315	23565

If you want to expand all the items of a field at once, do the following:

- Click on any of the items of the field – Region.

- Click the ANALYZE tab on the Ribbon.

- Click Expand Field in the Active Field group.

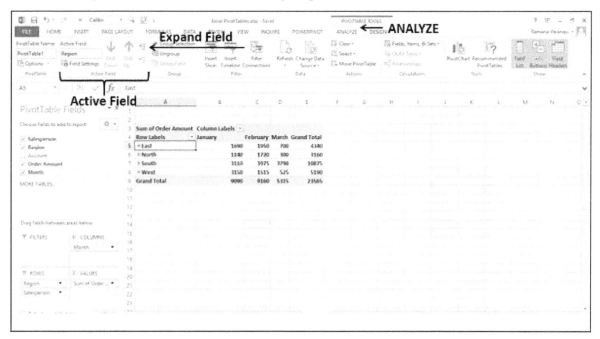

- All the items of the field Region will be expanded.

Grouping And Ungrouping Field Values

You can group and ungroup field values to define your clustering. For example, you might want to know the data combining East and North regions.

- Select the East and North items of the Region field in the PivotTable, along with the nested Salesperson field items.
- Click the ANALYZE tab on the Ribbon.
- Click Group Selection in the group – Group.

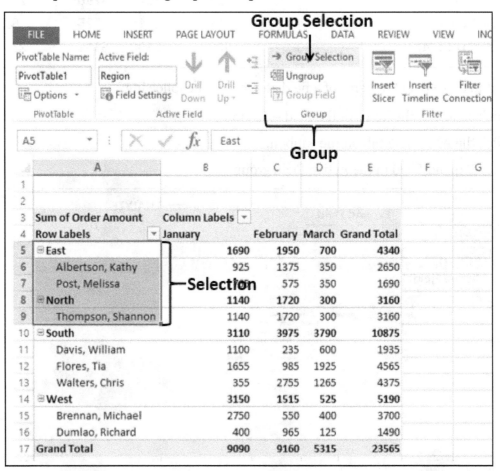

The items, East and North will be grouped under the named Group1. In addition, a new South is created under which the South is nested and a new West is created under which West is nested.

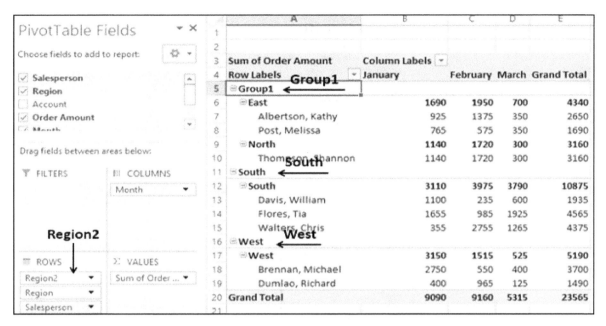

You can also observe that a new field – Region2 is added in the PivotTable Fields list, which appears in the ROWS area.

- Select the South and West items of the Region2 field in the PivotTable, along with the nested Region and Salesperson field items.
- Click the ANALYZE tab on the Ribbon.
- Click Group Selection in the group – Group.

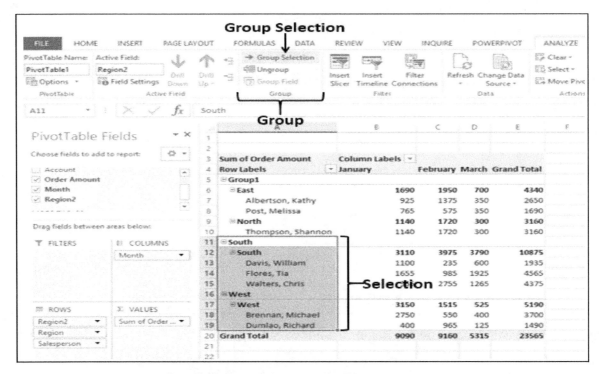

The items, South and West of the field Region will be grouped under the named Group2.

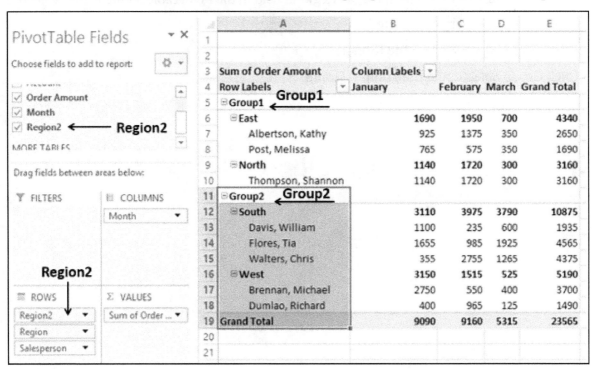

To ungroup a group, do the following:

- Click on the Group Name.

- Click the ANALYZE tab.
- Click Ungroup in the group – Group.

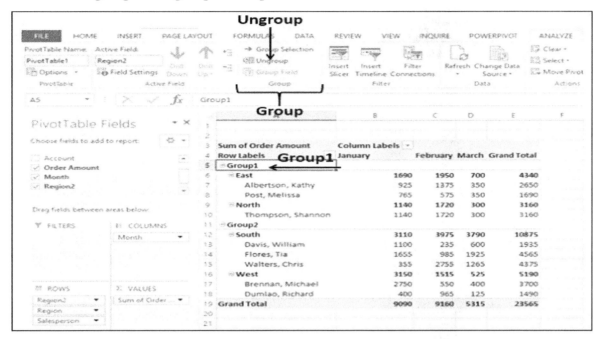

Grouping By A Date Field

Consider the following PivotTable, wherein you have the employee data summarized by Count of EmployeeID, hire date wise, and title wise.

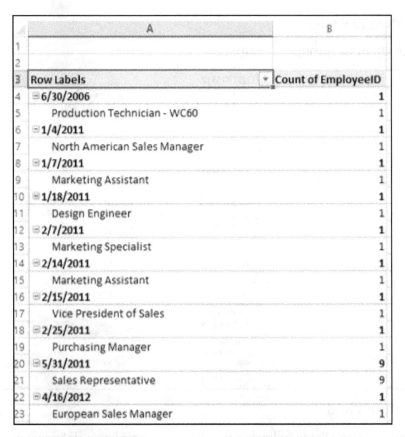

Row Labels	Count of EmployeeID
⊟ 6/30/2006	1
Production Technician - WC60	1
⊟ 1/4/2011	1
North American Sales Manager	1
⊟ 1/7/2011	1
Marketing Assistant	1
⊟ 1/18/2011	1
Design Engineer	1
⊟ 2/7/2011	1
Marketing Specialist	1
⊟ 2/14/2011	1
Marketing Assistant	1
⊟ 2/15/2011	1
Vice President of Sales	1
⊟ 2/25/2011	1
Purchasing Manager	1
⊟ 5/31/2011	9
Sales Representative	9
⊟ 4/16/2012	1
European Sales Manager	1

Suppose you want to group this data by the HireDate field that is a Date field into years and quarters.

- Click on a Date item in the PivotTable.
- Click the ANALYZE tab on the Ribbon.
- Click Group Field in the group – Group.

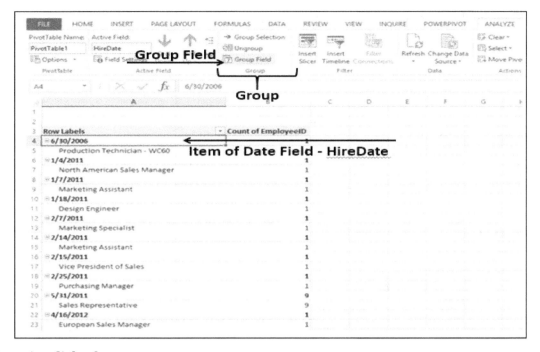

The Grouping dialog box appears.

- Set the dates for – Starting at and Ending at.
- Select Quarters and Years in the box under By. To select/deselect multiple items, keep the Ctrl-key pressed.
- Click OK.

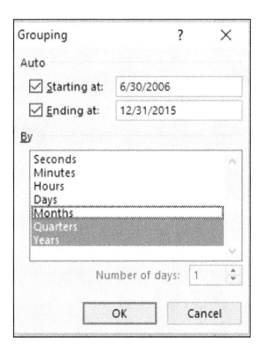

The HireDate field values will be grouped into Quarters, nested in Years. If you want to ungroup this grouping, you can do as shown earlier, by clicking Ungroup in the group – Group on the Ribbon.

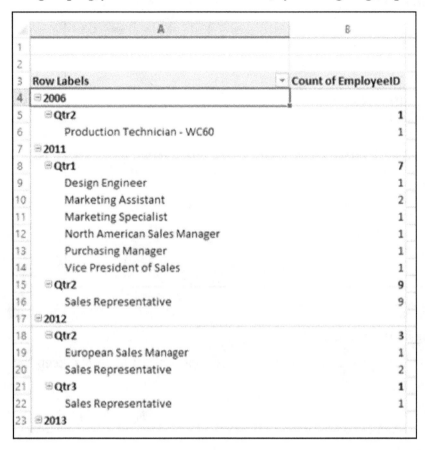

Row Labels	Count of EmployeeID
⊟ 2006	
⊟ Qtr2	1
Production Technician - WC60	1
⊟ 2011	
⊟ Qtr1	7
Design Engineer	1
Marketing Assistant	2
Marketing Specialist	1
North American Sales Manager	1
Purchasing Manager	1
Vice President of Sales	1
⊟ Qtr2	9
Sales Representative	9
⊟ 2012	
⊟ Qtr2	3
European Sales Manager	1
Sales Representative	2
⊟ Qtr3	1
Sales Representative	1
⊟ 2013	

Active Value Field Settings

You can set a field options by clicking on a value of that field. Consider the example of sales data that we used earlier in this chapter.

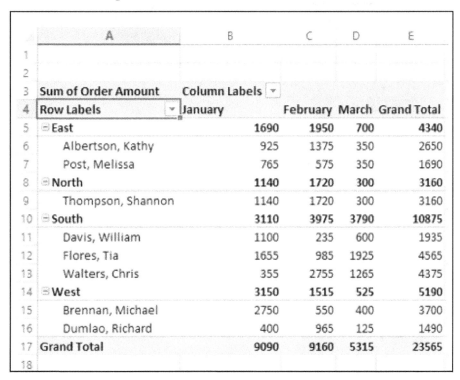

Sum of Order Amount	Column Labels ▾			
Row Labels ▾	January	February	March	Grand Total
⊟East	1690	1950	700	4340
Albertson, Kathy	925	1375	350	2650
Post, Melissa	765	575	350	1690
⊟North	1140	1720	300	3160
Thompson, Shannon	1140	1720	300	3160
⊟South	3110	3975	3790	10875
Davis, William	1100	235	600	1935
Flores, Tia	1655	985	1925	4565
Walters, Chris	355	2755	1265	4375
⊟West	3150	1515	525	5190
Brennan, Michael	2750	550	400	3700
Dumlao, Richard	400	965	125	1490
Grand Total	9090	9160	5315	23565

Suppose you want to set the options for the Region field.

- Click on East. On the Ribbon, in the Active Field group, in the Active Field box, Region will be displayed.
- Click on Field Settings. The Field Settings dialog box appears.

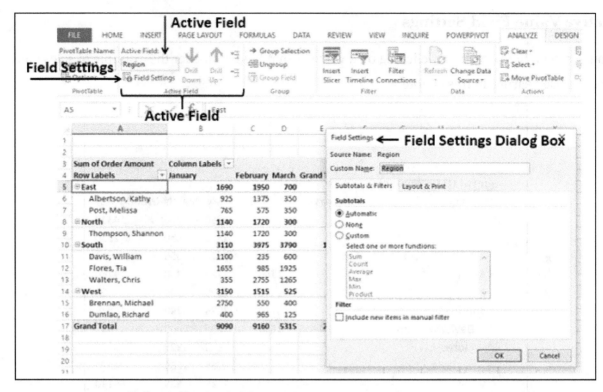

You can set your preferences for the field – Region.

PivotTable Options

You can set the PivotTable Options according to your preferences.

- Click on the PivotTable.
- Click the ANALYZE tab.
- Click Options in the PivotTable group.

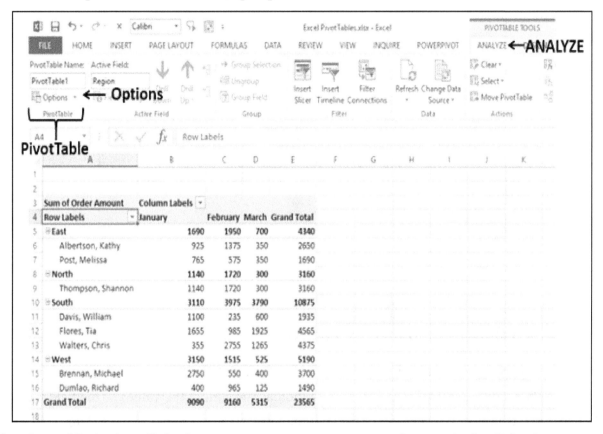

The PivotTable Options dialog box appears. You can set your preferences in the dialog box.

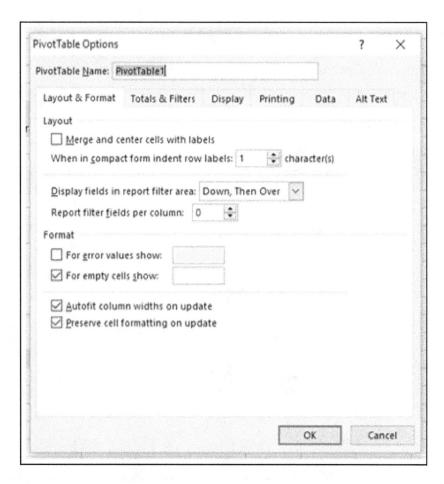

Excel Pivot Tables - Summarizing Values

You can summarize a PivotTable by placing a field in $\sum$ the VALUES area in the PivotTable Fields task pane. By default, Excel takes the summarization as the sum of the values of the field in $\sum$ the VALUES area. However, you have other calculation types, such as Count, Average, Max, Min, etc.

Sum

Consider the following PivotTable wherein you have the summarized sales data regionwise, salesperson-wise, and month-wise. As you can observe, when you drag the field Order Amount to $\sum$ VALUES area, it is displayed as Sum of Order Amount, indicating the calculation is taken as Sum. In the PivotTable, in the top-left corner, the Sum of Order Amount is displayed. Further, the Grand Total column and Grand Total row are displayed for subtotals field-wise in rows and columns respectively.

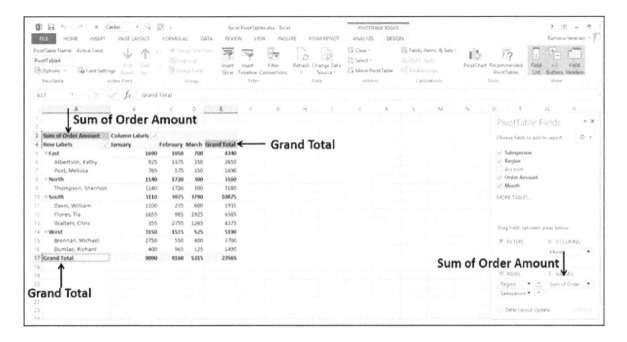

Value Field Settings

With Values Field Settings, you can set the calculation type in your PivotTable. You can also decide on how you want to display your values.

- Click on Sum of Order Amount in ∑ the VALUES area.
- Select Value Field Settings from the dropdown list.

The Value Field Settings dialog box appears.

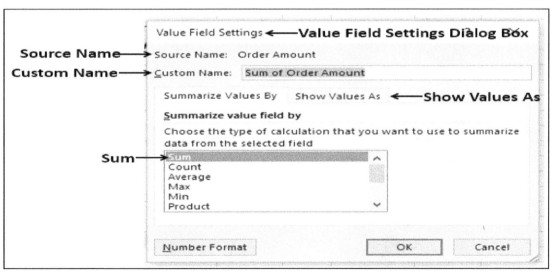

The Source Name is the field and Custom Name is the Sum of the field. The calculation Type is Sum. Click the Show Values As tab.

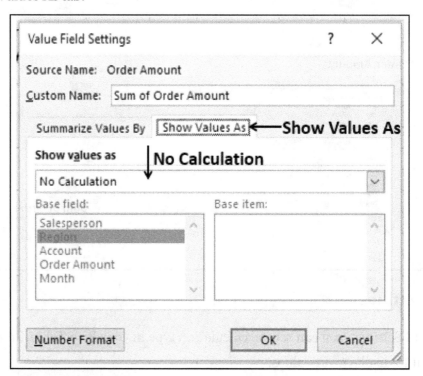

In the box Show Values As, No Calculation is displayed. Click the Show Values As box. You can find several ways of showing your total values.

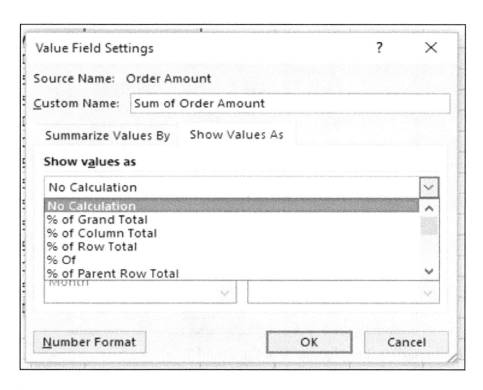

% Of Grand Total

You can show the values in the PivotTable as % of Grand Total.

- In the Custom Name box, type % of Grand Total.
- Click on the Show Values As box.
- Click on % of Grand Total in the dropdown list. Click OK.

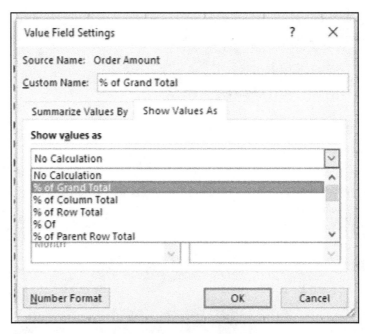

The PivotTable summarizes the values as % of the Grand Total.

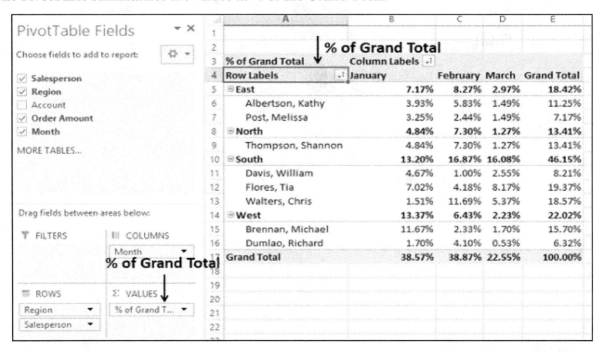

As you can observe, the Sum of Order Amount in the top-left corner of the PivotTable and the Σ VALUES area in the PivotTable Fields pane is changed to the new Custom Name - % of Grand Total.

- Click on the header of the Grand Total column.

- Type % of Grand Total in the formula bar. Both the Column and Row headers will change to % of Grand Total.

	A	B	C	D	E
1					
2					
3	% of Grand Total	Column Labels ⌄⌐			
4	Row Labels ⌄⌐	January	February	March	% of Grand Total
5	⊟East	7.17%	8.27%	2.97%	18.42%
6	Albertson, Kathy	3.93%	5.83%	1.49%	11.25%
7	Post, Melissa	3.25%	2.44%	1.49%	7.17%
8	⊟North	4.84%	7.30%	1.27%	13.41%
9	Thompson, Shannon	4.84%	7.30%	1.27%	13.41%
10	⊟South	13.20%	16.87%	16.08%	46.15%
11	Davis, William	4.67%	1.00%	2.55%	8.21%
12	Flores, Tia	7.02%	4.18%	8.17%	19.37%
13	Walters, Chris	1.51%	11.69%	5.37%	18.57%
14	⊟West	13.37%	6.43%	2.23%	22.02%
15	Brennan, Michael	11.67%	2.33%	1.70%	15.70%
16	Dumlao, Richard	1.70%	4.10%	0.53%	6.32%
17	% of Grand Total	38.57%	38.87%	22.55%	100.00%

% Of Column Total

Suppose you want to summarize the values as % of each month's total.

- Click on Sum of Order Amount in ∑ the VALUES area.
- Select Value Field Settings from the dropdown list. The Value Field Settings dialog box appears.
- In the Custom Name box, type % of Month Total.
- Click on the Show values as a box.
- Select % of Column Total from the dropdown list.
- Click OK.

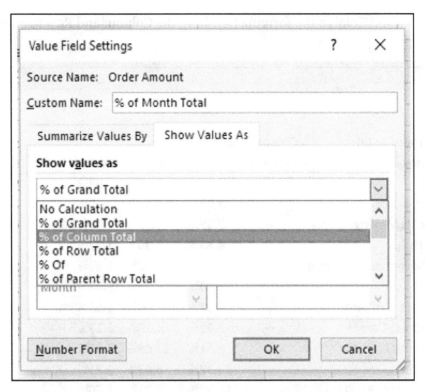

The PivotTable summarizes the values as % of the Column Total. In the Month columns, you will find the values as % of the specific month total.

- Click on the header of the Grand Total column.

- Type % of Column Total in the formula bar. Both the Column and Row headers will change to % of Column Total.

% of Month Total	Column Labels			
Row Labels	January	February	March	% of Column Total
⊟East	18.59%	21.29%	13.17%	18.42%
Albertson, Kathy	10.18%	15.01%	6.59%	11.25%
Post, Melissa	8.42%	6.28%	6.59%	7.17%
⊟North	12.54%	18.78%	5.64%	13.41%
Thompson, Shannon	12.54%	18.78%	5.64%	13.41%
⊟South	34.21%	43.40%	71.31%	46.15%
Davis, William	12.10%	2.57%	11.29%	8.21%
Flores, Tia	18.21%	10.75%	36.22%	19.37%
Walters, Chris	3.91%	30.08%	23.80%	18.57%
⊟West	34.65%	16.54%	9.88%	22.02%
Brennan, Michael	30.25%	6.00%	7.53%	15.70%
Dumlao, Richard	4.40%	10.53%	2.35%	6.32%
% of Column Total	100.00%	100.00%	100.00%	100.00%

% Of Row Total

You can summarize the values as % of region totals and % of salesperson totals, by selecting % of Row Total in the Show Values As box in the Value Field Settings dialog box.

	A	B	C	D	E
1					
2					
3	% of Row Total	Column Labels			
4	Row Labels	January	February	March	% of Row Total
5	⊟East	38.94%	44.93%	16.13%	100.00%
6	Albertson, Kathy	34.91%	51.89%	13.21%	100.00%
7	Post, Melissa	45.27%	34.02%	20.71%	100.00%
8	⊟North	36.08%	54.43%	9.49%	100.00%
9	Thompson, Shannon	36.08%	54.43%	9.49%	100.00%
10	⊟South	28.60%	36.55%	34.85%	100.00%
11	Davis, William	56.85%	12.14%	31.01%	100.00%
12	Flores, Tia	36.25%	21.58%	42.17%	100.00%
13	Walters, Chris	8.11%	62.97%	28.91%	100.00%
14	⊟West	60.69%	29.19%	10.12%	100.00%
15	Brennan, Michael	74.32%	14.86%	10.81%	100.00%
16	Dumlao, Richard	26.85%	64.77%	8.39%	100.00%
17	% of Row Total	38.57%	38.87%	22.55%	100.00%

Count

Suppose you want to summarize the values by the number of Accounts region-wise, salesperson wise and month-wise.

- Deselect Order Amount.
- Drag Account to $\sum$ VALUES area. The Sum of the Account will be displayed in the $\sum$ VALUES area.
- Click on Sum of Account.
- Select Value Field Settings from the dropdown list. The Value Field Settings dialog box appears.
- In the Summarize value field by box, select Count. The Custom Name changes to Count of Account.
- Click OK.

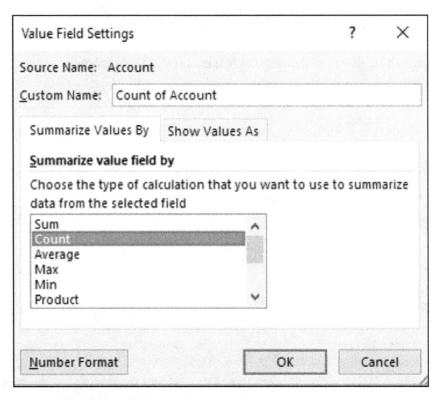

The Count of Account will be displayed as shown below:

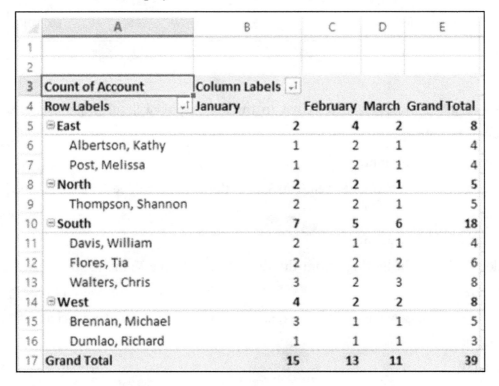

	January	February	March	Grand Total
East	2	4	2	8
Albertson, Kathy	1	2	1	4
Post, Melissa	1	2	1	4
North	2	2	1	5
Thompson, Shannon	2	2	1	5
South	7	5	6	18
Davis, William	2	1	1	4
Flores, Tia	2	2	2	6
Walters, Chris	3	2	3	8
West	4	2	2	8
Brennan, Michael	3	1	1	5
Dumlao, Richard	1	1	1	3
Grand Total	15	13	11	39

Average

Suppose you want to summarize the PivotTable by average values of Order Amount region-wise, salesperson-wise, and month-wise.

- Deselect Account.
- Drag Order Amount to $\sum$ VALUES area. The Sum of Order Amount will be displayed in the $\sum$ VALUES area.
- Click on Sum of Order Amount.
- Click on Value Field Settings in the dropdown list. The Value Field Settings dialog box appears.
- In the Summarize value field by box, click on Average. The Custom Name changes to Average of Order Amount.
- Click OK.

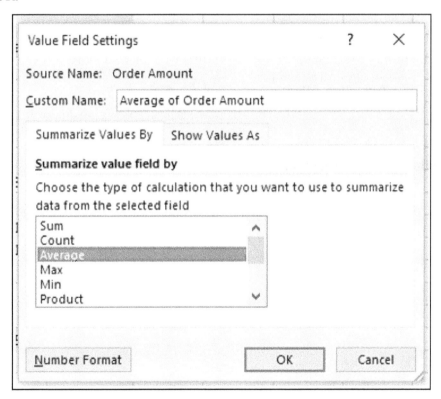

The average will be displayed as shown below:

	A	B	C	D	E
1					
2					
3	**Average of Order Amount**	**Column Labels** ⏷			
4	**Row Labels** ⏷	**January**	**February**	**March**	**Grand Total**
5	⊟ **East**	845	487.5	350	542.5
6	Albertson, Kathy	925	687.5	350	662.5
7	Post, Melissa	765	287.5	350	422.5
8	⊟ **North**	570	860	300	632
9	Thompson, Shannon	570	860	300	632
10	⊟ **South**	444.2857143	795	631.6666667	604.1666667
11	Davis, William	550	235	600	483.75
12	Flores, Tia	827.5	492.5	962.5	760.8333333
13	Walters, Chris	118.3333333	1377.5	421.6666667	546.875
14	⊟ **West**	787.5	757.5	262.5	648.75
15	Brennan, Michael	916.6666667	550	400	740
16	Dumlao, Richard	400	965	125	496.6666667
17	**Grand Total**	606	704.6153846	483.1818182	604.2307692

You have to set the number format of the values in the PivotTable to make it more presentable.

- Click on Average of Order Amount in Σ VALUES area.
- Click on Value Field Settings in the dropdown list. The Value Field Settings dialog box appears.
- Click on the Number Format button.

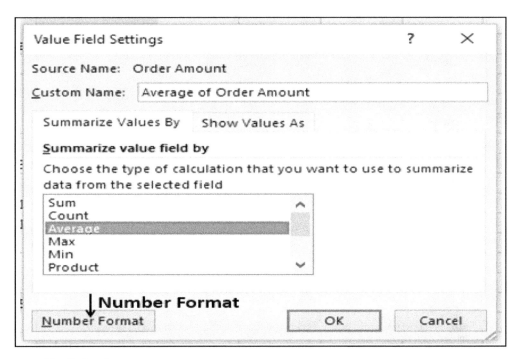

The Format Cells dialog box appears.

- Click on Number under Category.
- Type 2 in the Decimal places box and click OK.

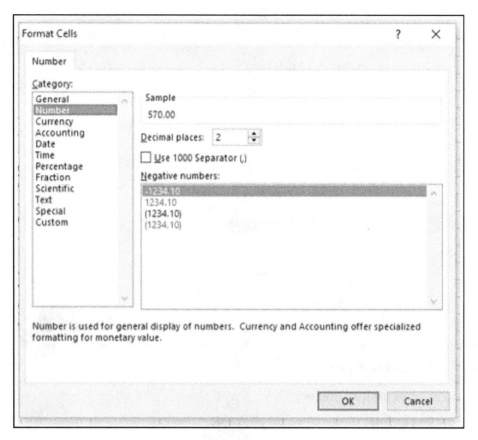

- The PivotTable values will be formatted to numbers with two decimal places.

Average of Order Amount	Column Labels ▾ᴵ			
Row Labels ▾ᴵ	January	February	March	Grand Total
⊟East	845.00	487.50	350.00	542.50
Albertson, Kathy	925.00	687.50	350.00	662.50
Post, Melissa	765.00	287.50	350.00	422.50
⊟North	570.00	860.00	300.00	632.00
Thompson, Shannon	570.00	860.00	300.00	632.00
⊟South	444.29	795.00	631.67	604.17
Davis, William	550.00	235.00	600.00	483.75
Flores, Tia	827.50	492.50	962.50	760.83
Walters, Chris	118.33	1377.50	421.67	546.88
⊟West	787.50	757.50	262.50	648.75
Brennan, Michael	916.67	550.00	400.00	740.00
Dumlao, Richard	400.00	965.00	125.00	496.67
Grand Total	606.00	704.62	483.18	604.23

- Click on the header of the Grand Total column.
- Type Average Order Amount in the formula bar. Both the Column and Row headers will change to Average Order Amount.

	A	B	C	D	E
1					
2					
3	**Average of Order Amount**	**Column Labels**			
4	**Row Labels**	**January**	**February**	**March**	**Average Order Amount**
5	⊟ **East**	845.00	487.50	350.00	542.50
6	Albertson, Kathy	925.00	687.50	350.00	662.50
7	Post, Melissa	765.00	287.50	350.00	422.50
8	⊟ **North**	570.00	860.00	300.00	632.00
9	Thompson, Shannon	570.00	860.00	300.00	632.00
10	⊟ **South**	444.29	795.00	631.67	604.17
11	Davis, William	550.00	235.00	600.00	483.75
12	Flores, Tia	827.50	492.50	962.50	760.83
13	Walters, Chris	118.33	1377.50	421.67	546.88
14	⊟ **West**	787.50	757.50	262.50	648.75
15	Brennan, Michael	916.67	550.00	400.00	740.00
16	Dumlao, Richard	400.00	965.00	125.00	496.67
17	**Average Order Amount**	606.00	704.62	483.18	604.23

Max

Suppose you want to summarize the PivotTable by the maximum values of Order Amount region-wise, salesperson-wise and month-wise.

- Click on Sum of Order Amount.
- Select Value Field Settings from the dropdown list. The Value Field Settings dialog box appears.
- In the Summarize value field by box, click Max. The Custom Name changes to Max of Order Amount.

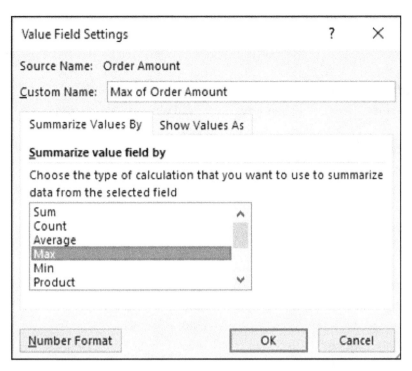

The PivotTable will display the region of the maximum value-wise, salesperson-wise, and month-wise.

- Click on the header of the Grand Total column.
- Type Max Order Amount in the formula bar. Both the Column and Row headers will change to Max Order Amount.

	A	B	C	D	E
1					
2					
3	Max of Order Amount	Column Labels ⌄			
4	Row Labels ⌄	January	February	March	Max Order Amount
5	⊟East	925	875	350	925
6	Albertson, Kathy	925	875	350	925
7	Post, Melissa	765	425	350	765
8	⊟North	875	1345	300	1345
9	Thompson, Shannon	875	1345	300	1345
10	⊟South	1350	2600	1500	2600
11	Davis, William	850	235	600	850
12	Flores, Tia	1350	550	1500	1500
13	Walters, Chris	225	2600	785	2600
14	⊟West	1500	965	400	1500
15	Brennan, Michael	1500	550	400	1500
16	Dumlao, Richard	400	965	125	965
17	Max Order Amount	1500	2600	1500	2600

Min

Suppose you want to summarize the PivotTable by the minimum values of Order Amount region-wise, salesperson-wise, and month-wise.

- Click on Sum of Order Amount.
- Click on Value Field Settings in the dropdown list. The Value Field Settings dialog box appears.
- In the Summarize value field by box, click Min. The Custom Name changes to Min of Order Amount.

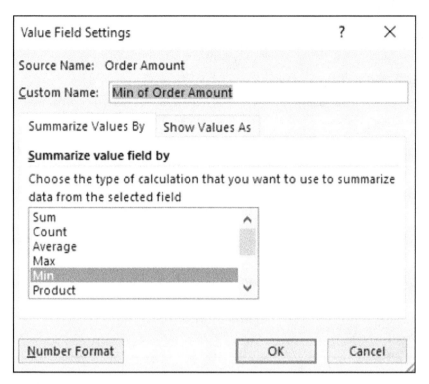

The PivotTable will display the region of the minimum value-wise, salesperson-wise, and month-wise.

- Click on the header of the Grand Total column.
- Type Min Order Amount in the formula bar. Both the Column and Row headers will change to Min Order Amount.

	A	B	C	D	E
1					
2					
3	**Min of Order Amount**	Column Labels ⤵			
4	**Row Labels** ⤵	January	February	March	Min Order Amount
5	⊟ **East**	765	150	350	150
6	Albertson, Kathy	925	500	350	350
7	Post, Melissa	765	150	350	150
8	⊟ **North**	265	375	300	265
9	Thompson, Shannon	265	375	300	265
10	⊟ **South**	25	155	225	25
11	Davis, William	250	235	600	235
12	Flores, Tia	305	435	425	305
13	Walters, Chris	25	155	225	25
14	⊟ **West**	400	550	125	125
15	Brennan, Michael	400	550	400	400
16	Dumlao, Richard	400	965	125	125
17	**Min Order Amount**	25	150	125	25

CHAPTER 8: EXCEL CHARTING BASICS

What Are Graphs And Charts In Excel?

Charts and graphs elevate your data by providing an easy-to-understand visualization of numeric values. While the terms are often used interchangeably, they are slightly different. Graphs are the most basic way to represent data visually, and typically display data point values over a duration of time. Charts are a bit more complex, as they allow you to compare pieces of a data set relative to the other data in that set. Charts are also considered more visual than graphs since they often take a different shape than a generic x- and y-axis.

People often use charts and graphs in presentations to give management, client, or team members a quick snapshot into progress or results. You can create a chart or graph to represent nearly any kind of quantitative data, doing so will save you the time and frustration of poring through spreadsheets to find relationships and trends.

It's easy to create charts and graphs in Excel, especially since you can also store your data directly in an Excel Workbook, rather than importing data from another program. Excel also has a variety of preset chart and graph types so you can select one that best represents the data relationship(s) you want to highlight.

Explanation of Charts

A chart is a tool you can use in Excel to communicate data graphically. Charts allow your audience to see the meaning behind the numbers, and they make showing comparisons and trends much easier.

In this book, you will learn how to insert charts and modify them so they communicate information effectively. Each of Excel's 12 chart types has different features that make them better suited for specific tasks. Pairing a chart with its correct data-style will make the information easier to understand, enhancing the communication within your small business.

Graphs or charts help people understand data quickly. Whether you want to make a comparison, show a relationship, or highlight a trend, they help your audience "see" what you are talking about.

Among its many features, Microsoft Excel enables you to incorporate charts, providing a way to add visual appeal to your business reports.

The Importance of Charts

- Allows you to visualize data graphically
- It's easier to analyze trends and patterns using charts in MS Excel
- Easy to interpret compared to data in cells

When To Use Each Chart And Graph Type In Excel

Excel offers a large library of chart and graph types to help visually present your data. While multiple chart types might "work" for a given data set, it's important to select a chart type that best fits with the story you want the data to tell. Of course, you can also add graphical elements to enhance and customize a chart or graph. In Excel 2016, there are five main categories of charts or graphs:

- Excel provides you with different types of charts that suit your purpose. Based on the type of data, you can create a chart. You can also change the chart type later.

Excel Offers The Following Major Chart Types:

- Column Chart
- Line Chart
- Pie Chart
- Doughnut Chart
- Bar Chart
- Area Chart
- XY (Scatter) Chart
- Bubble Chart
- Stock Chart
- Surface Chart
- Radar Chart
- Combo Chart

Each of these chart types has sub-types. In this book, you will have an overview of the different chart types and get to know the sub-types for each chart type.

1. Column Chart

A Column Chart typically displays the categories along with the horizontal (category) axis and values along with the vertical (value) axis. To create a column chart, arrange the data in columns or rows on the worksheet. A column chart has the following sub-types:

- Clustered Column.
- Stacked Column.
- 100% Stacked Column.
- 3-D Clustered Column.
- 3-D Stacked Column.
- 3-D 100% Stacked Column.
- 3-D Column.

2. Line Chart

Line charts can show continuous data over time on an evenly scaled axis. Therefore, they are ideal for showing trends in data at equal intervals, such as months, quarters, or years. In a Line chart:

- Category data is distributed evenly along the horizontal axis.
- Value data is distributed evenly along the vertical axis.
- To create a Line chart, arrange the data in columns or rows on the worksheet.

A-Line Chart Has The Following Sub-Types:

- Line
- Stacked Line
- 100% Stacked Line
- Line with Markers
- Stacked Line with Markers
- 100% Stacked Line with Markers
- 3-D Line

3. Pie Chart

Pie charts show the size of items in one data series, proportional to the sum of the items. The data points in a pie chart are shown as a percentage of the whole pie. To create a Pie Chart, arrange the data in one column or row on the worksheet. A Pie Chart has the following sub-types:

- Pie

- 3-D Pie
- Pie of Pie
- Bar of Pie

4. Doughnut Chart

A Doughnut chart shows the relationship of parts to a whole. It is similar to a Pie Chart with the only difference that a Doughnut Chart can contain more than one data series, whereas, a Pie Chart can contain only one data series.

A Doughnut Chart contains rings and each ring represents one data series. To create a Doughnut Chart, arrange the data in columns or rows on a worksheet.

5. Bar Chart

Bar Charts illustrate comparisons among individual items. In a Bar Chart, the categories are organized along the vertical axis and the values are organized along the horizontal axis. To create a Bar Chart, arrange the data in columns or rows on the Worksheet. A Bar Chart has the following sub-types:

- Clustered Bar
- Stacked Bar
- 100% Stacked Bar
- 3-D Clustered Bar
- 3-D Stacked Bar
- 3-D 100% Stacked Bar

6. Area Chart

Area Charts can be used to plot the change over time and draw attention to the total value across a trend. By showing the sum of the plotted values, an area chart also shows the relationship of parts to a whole. To create an Area Chart, arrange the data in columns or rows on the worksheet. An Area Chart has the following sub-types:

- Area
- Stacked Area
- 100% Stacked Area
- 3-D Area
- 3-D Stacked Area

- 3-D 100% Stacked Area

7. XY (Scatter) Chart

XY (Scatter) charts are typically used for showing and comparing numeric values, like scientific, statistical, and engineering data.

A Scatter Chart Has Two Value Axes:

Horizontal (x) Value Axis

Vertical (y) Value Axis

It combines x and y values into single data points and displays them in irregular intervals, or clusters. To create a Scatter chart, arrange the data in columns and rows on the worksheet.

Place the x values in one row or column, and then enter the corresponding y values in the adjacent rows or columns.

Consider Using A Scatter Chart When:

- You want to change the scale of the horizontal axis.
- You want to make that axis a logarithmic scale.
- Values for the horizontal axis are not evenly spaced.
- There are many data points on the horizontal axis.
- You want to adjust the independent axis scales of a scatter chart to reveal more information about data that includes pairs or grouped sets of values.
- You want to show similarities between large sets of data instead of differences between data points.
- You want to compare many data points regardless of the time.
- The more data that you include in a scatter chart, the better the comparisons you can make.

A Scatter Chart Has The Following Sub-Types:

- Scatter
- Scatter with Smooth Lines and Markers
- Scatter with Smooth Lines
- Scatter with Straight Lines and Markers
- Scatter with Straight Lines

8. Bubble Chart

A Bubble chart is like a Scatter chart with an additional third column to specify the size of the bubbles it shows to represent the data points in the data series. A Bubble chart has the following sub-types:

- Bubble
- Bubble with 3-D effect

9. Stock Chart

As the name implies, stock charts can show fluctuations in stock prices. However, a Stock chart can also be used to show fluctuations in other data, such as daily rainfall or annual temperatures. To create a Stock chart, arrange the data in columns or rows in a specific order on the worksheet. For example, to create a simple high-low-close Stock chart, arrange your data with High, Low, and Close entered as column headings, in that order. A Stock chart has the following sub-types:

- High-Low-Close
- Open-High-Low-Close
- Volume-High-Low-Close
- Volume-Open-High-Low-Close

10. Surface Chart

A Surface chart is useful when you want to find the optimum combinations between two sets of data. As in a topographic map, colors and patterns indicate areas that are in the same range of values. To create a Surface chart:

- Ensure that both the categories and the data series are numeric values.
- Arrange the data in columns or rows on the worksheet.

A Surface Chart Has The Following Sub-Types:

- 3-D Surface
- Wireframe 3-D Surface
- Contour
- Wireframe Contour

11. Radar Chart

Radar charts compare the aggregate values of several data series. To create a Radar chart, arrange the data in columns or rows on the worksheet. A Radar chart has the following sub-types:

- Radar
- Radar with Markers
- Filled Radar

12. Combo Chart

Combo charts combine two or more chart types to make the data easy to understand, especially when the data is widely varied. It is shown with a secondary axis and is even easier to read. To create a Combo chart, arrange the data in columns and rows on the worksheet. A Combo chart has the following sub-types:

- Clustered Column – Line
- Clustered Column – Line on Secondary Axis
- Stacked Area – Clustered Column
- Custom Combination

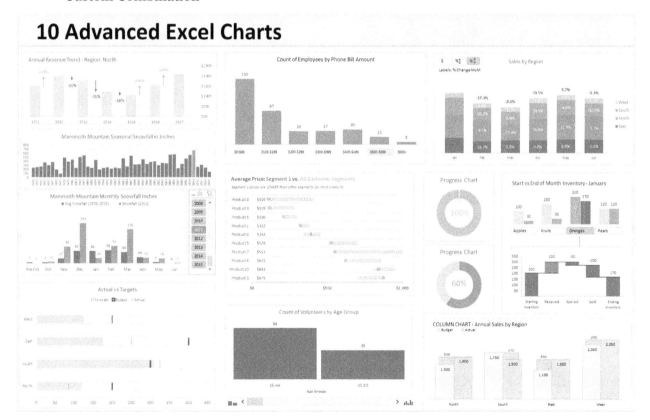

Types of Graphs In Excel

We have seen multiple uses of excel in our professional lives; it helps us analyze, sort, and extract insights from data. There is one feature of excel that helps us put insights gained from our data into a visual form. This feature helps us display data in an easy-to-understand pictorial format. We are talking about graphs in excel. Excel supports most of the commonly used graphs in statistics.

Creating different types of graphs in excel according to our data is very easy and convenient when it comes to analysis, comparing datasets, presentations, etc. In this article, we will discuss the six most commonly used types of graphs in excel. We will also discuss how to select the correct graph type for some kinds of data.

Common Types Of Graphs In Excel

The most common types of graphs used in Excel are:

- Pie Graph
- Column Graph
- Line Graph
- Area Graph
- Scatter Graph

Let's understand what the different types of graphs in Excel are and how to create them. We will start with a few examples of types of graphs in Excel.

1. The Pie Graph

As the name suggests, the pie graph is a display of data in the form of a pie or circle. This graph type is used for showing the proportions of a whole. For example, if we want to compare who did how much work in a team, we would use a pie graph to display it in an easy way to understand.

2. The Column Or Bar Graph

The next one in the list is a column graph, also called a bar graph in statistics. We use these different types of graphs where we need to see and compare values across a range. The same data that we used in the pie graph example would look like this:

There are different types of bar graphs available in Excel, such as stacked columns, 100% stacked columns, 3D columns, etc. These types of graphs can be used for expanded datasets. For example, we have been working with only two columns in the last two examples, now; if we want to include the hours worked as a third column and compare the hours worked with the number of datasets visually, we can either use a stacked column or a 100% stacked column which would look like this:

The difference between these is that while a stacked column represents actual values, a 100% stacked column represents the values as percentages. There are 3D versions as well as horizontal versions of these graphs in excel.

3. The Line Graph

The next type of graph we are going to discuss is called a line graph. This type of graph is used when we need to visualize data like an increasing or decreasing series over a period. This is an excellent graph in Excel to use for representing trends and comparing performance. For example, if we wanted to see how the current rise compares to the last raise for different people in the earlier examples, we would get something like this:

4. The Area Graph

The area graph is available within the line graph menu. This is used for the same purpose as the line graph, which visualizes trends and compares data. In this example, we represent the relationship between the number of datasets worked on by an analyst and the number of hours they worked. The stacked area graph on the right is used for drawing attention to the difference in magnitude of two categories and displays the values as percentages.

5. The Scatter Graph

The Scatter graph is a simple representation of data points in excel. It is used when we need to compare at least two sets of data with a limited number of data points.

There are many more types of graphs available in Excel, such as Hierarchy graph, Radar graph, Waterfall graph, and Combo graphs which are combinations of two or more graphs. All these are used based on specific conditions fulfilled by the data, such as the type of data, the number of data points, etc.

Things To Remember About Types Of Graphs In Excel

Know your data before making a graph. A type of graph that may suit a time series may not be suitable for a set of unpatterned data.

- Sort the data before making graphs.
- Do not use unnecessary styling while making the graph.

How To Chart Data In Excel

To generate a chart or graph in Excel, you must first provide Excel with data to pull from. In this section, we'll show you how to chart data in Excel 2016.

Step 1: Enter Data Into A Worksheet

- Open Excel and select New Workbook.
- Enter the data you want to use to create a graph or chart. In this example, we're comparing the profit of five different products from 2013 to 2017. Be sure to include labels for your columns and rows. Doing so enables you to translate the data into a chart or graph with clear axis labels.

	A	B	C	D	E	F
1	Product ▼	2013 ▼	2014 ▼	2015 ▼	2016 ▼	2017 ▼
2	Product A	$18,580	$49,225	$16,326	$10,017	$26,134
3	Product B	$78,970	$82,262	$48,640	$48,640	$48,640
4	Product C	$24,236	$131,390	$79,022	$71,009	$81,474
5	Product D	$16,730	$19,730	$12,109	$11,355	$17,686
6	Product E	$35,358	$42,685	$20,893	$16,065	$21,388
7						

Step 2: Select Range To Create Chart Or Graph From Workbook Data

- Highlight the cells that contain the data you want to use in your graph by clicking and dragging your mouse across the cells.
- Your cell range will now be highlighted in gray and you can select a chart type.

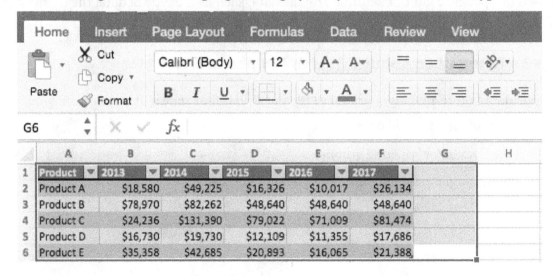

How To Make A Chart In Excel

Once you input your data and select the cell range, you're ready to choose your chart type to display your data. In this example, we'll create a clustered column chart from the data we used in the previous section.

Step 1: Select Chart Type

Once your data is highlighted in the Workbook, click the Insert tab on the top banner. About halfway across the toolbar is a section with several chart options. Excel provides Recommended Charts based on popularity, but you can click any of the dropdown menus to select a different template.

Step 2: Create Your Chart

- From the Insert tab, click the column chart icon and select Clustered Column.

- Excel will automatically create a clustered chart column from your selected data. The chart will appear in the center of your workbook.
- To name your chart, double click the Chart Title text in the chart and type a title. We'll call this chart "Product Profit 2013 - 2017."

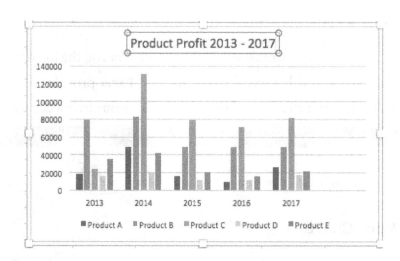

COLUMN CHART TEMPLATE

PRODUCT	2013	2014	2015	2016	2017
Product A	$18,580	$49,225	$16,326	$10,017	$26,134
Product B	$78,970	$82,262	$48,640	$48,640	$48,640
Product C	$24,236	$131,390	$79,022	$71,009	$81,474
Product D	$16,730	$19,730	$12,109	$11,355	$17,686
Product E	$35,358	$42,685	$20,893	$16,065	$21,388

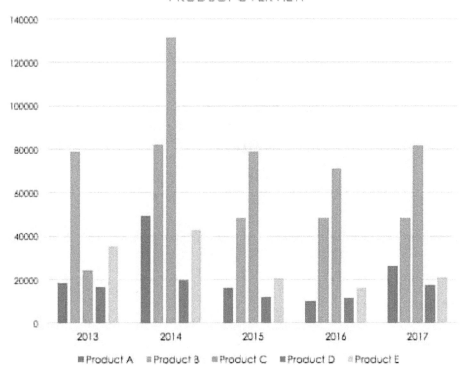

PRODUCT OVERVIEW

There are two tabs on the toolbar that you will use to make adjustments to your chart: Chart Design and Format. Excel automatically applies design, layout, and format presets to charts and graphs, but you can add customization by exploring the tabs. Next, we'll walk you through all the available adjustments in Chart Design.

Step 3: Add Chart Elements

Adding chart elements to your chart or graph will enhance it by clarifying data or providing additional context. You can select a chart element by clicking on the Add Chart Element dropdown menu in the top left-hand corner (beneath the Home tab).

To Display Or Hide Axes:

- Select Axes. Excel will automatically pull the column and row headers from your selected cell range to display both horizontal and vertical axes on your chart (Under Axes, there is a checkmark next to Primary Horizontal and Primary Vertical.)

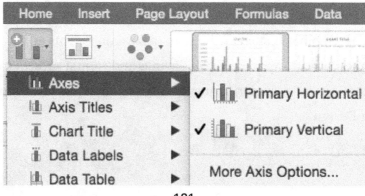

- Uncheck these options to remove the display axis on your chart. In this example, clicking Primary Horizontal will remove the year labels on the horizontal axis of your chart.

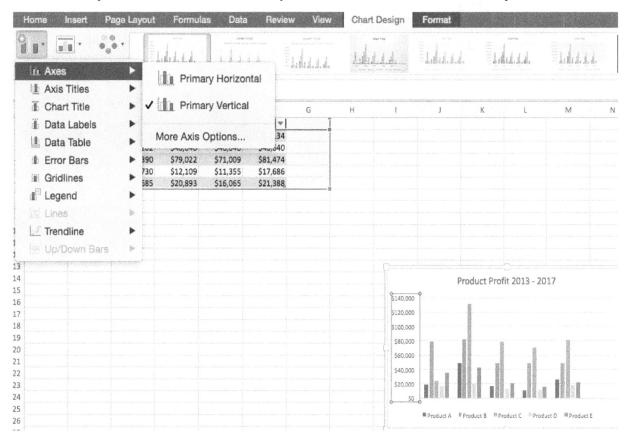

- Click More Axis Options... from the Axes dropdown menu to open a window with additional formatting and text options such as adding tick marks, labels, or numbers, or to change text color and size.

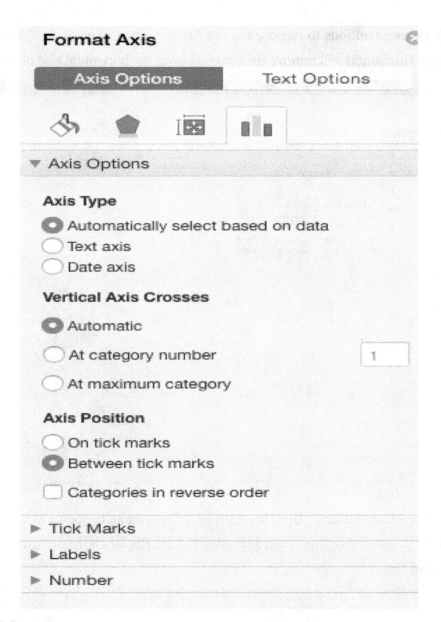

To Add Axis Titles:
- Click Add Chart Element and click Axis Titles from the dropdown menu. Excel will not automatically add axis titles to your chart; therefore, both Primary Horizontal and Primary Vertical will be unchecked.

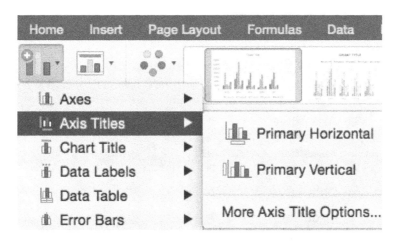

- To create axis titles, click Primary Horizontal or Primary Vertical and a text box will appear on the chart. We clicked both in this example. Type your axis titles. In this example, we added the titles "Year" (horizontal) and "Profit" (vertical).

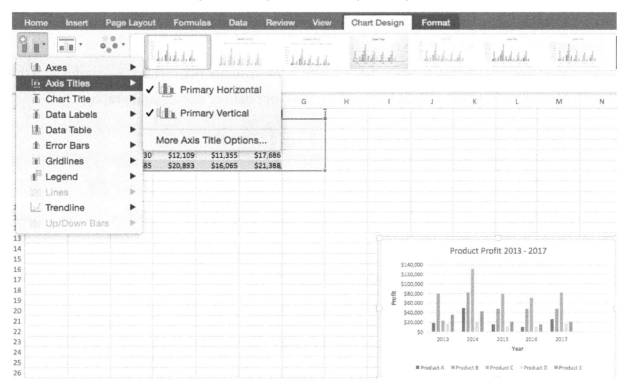

To Remove Or Move Chart Title:

- Click Add Chart Element and click Chart Title. You will see four options: None, Above Chart, Centered Overlay, and More Title Options.

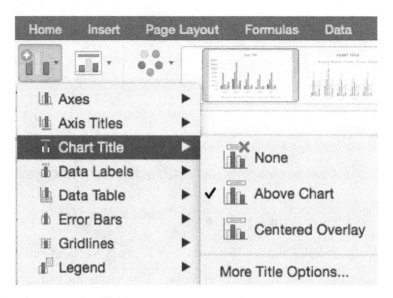

- Click None to remove the chart title.
- Click the Above Chart to place the title above the chart. If you create a chart title, Excel will automatically place it above the chart.
- Click Centered Overlay to place the title within the gridlines of the chart. Be careful with this option: you don't want the title to cover any of your data or clutter your graph.

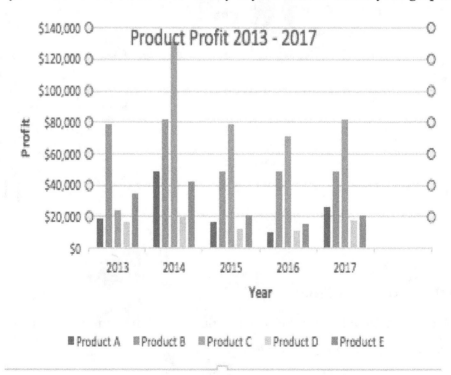

To Add Data Labels:

- Click Add Chart Element and click Data Labels. There are six options for data labels: None (default), Center, Inside End, Inside Base, Outside End, and More Data Label Title Options.

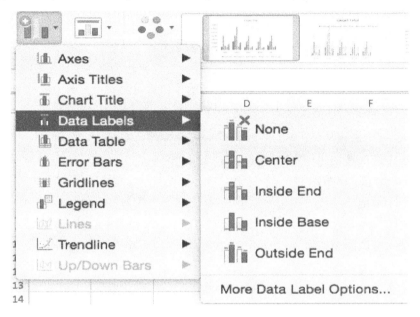

- The four placement options will add specific labels to each data point measured in your chart. Click the option you want. This customization can be helpful if you have a small amount of precise data, or if you have a lot of extra space in your chart. For a clustered column chart, however, adding data labels will likely look too cluttered.

To Add A Data Table:

- Click Add Chart Element and click Data Table. There are three pre-formatted options along with an extended menu that can be found by clicking More Data Table Options:

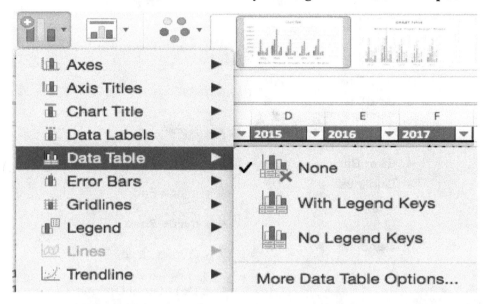

- None is the default setting, where the data table is not duplicated within the chart.
- With Legend Keys displays the data table beneath the chart to show the data range. The color-coded legend will also be included.

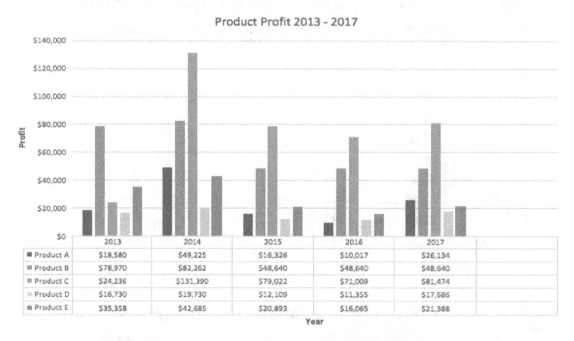

- No Legend Keys also displays the data table beneath the chart, but without the legend.

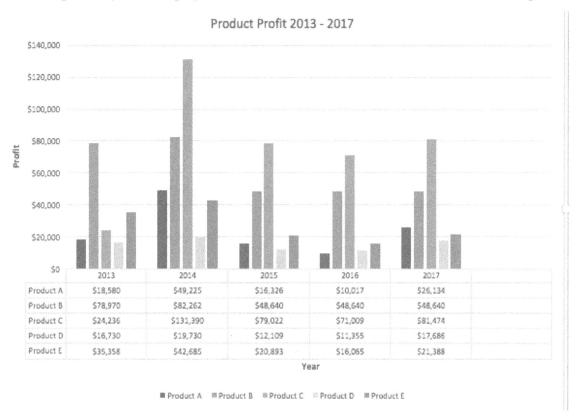

Product Profit 2013 - 2017

	2013	2014	2015	2016	2017
Product A	$18,580	$49,225	$16,326	$10,017	$26,134
Product B	$78,970	$82,262	$48,640	$48,640	$48,640
Product C	$24,236	$131,390	$79,022	$71,009	$81,474
Product D	$16,730	$19,730	$12,109	$11,355	$17,686
Product E	$35,358	$42,685	$20,893	$16,065	$21,388

■ Product A ■ Product B ■ Product C ■ Product D ■ Product E

Note: If you choose to include a data table, you'll probably want to make your chart larger to accommodate the table. Simply click the corner of your chart and use drag-and-drop to resize your chart.

To Add Error Bars:

- Click Add Chart Element and click Error Bars. In addition to More Error Bars Options, there are four options: None (default), Standard Error, 5% (Percentage), and Standard Deviation. Adding error bars provide a visual representation of the potential error in the shown data, based on different standard equations for isolating error.

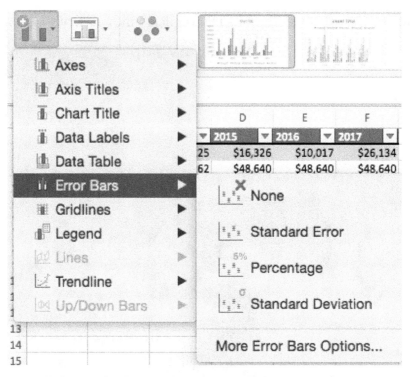

For example, when we click Standard Error from the options we get a chart

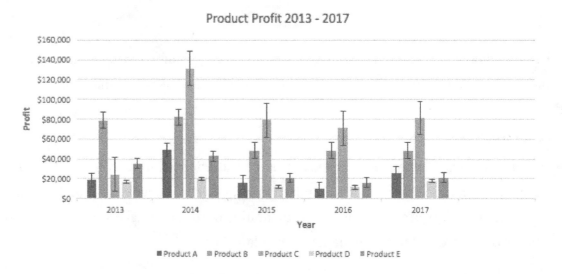

To Add Gridlines:

- Click Add Chart Element and click Gridlines. In addition to More Grid Line Options, there are four options: Primary Major Horizontal, Primary Major Vertical, Primary Minor Horizontal, and Primary Minor Vertical. For a column chart, Excel will add Primary Major Horizontal gridlines by default.

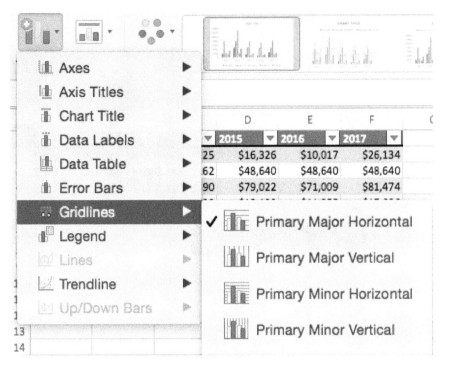

- You can select as many different gridlines as you want by clicking the options. For example, here is what our chart looks like when we click all four gridline options.

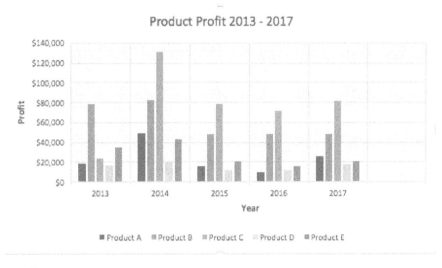

To Add A Legend:

- Click Add Chart Element and click Legend. In addition to More Legend Options, there are five options for legend placement: None, Right, Top, Left, and Bottom.

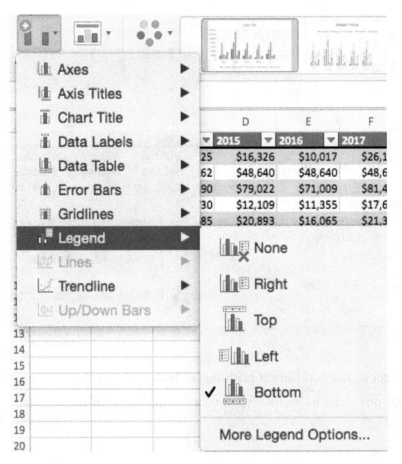

- Legend placement will depend on the style and format of your chart. Check the option that looks best on your chart.

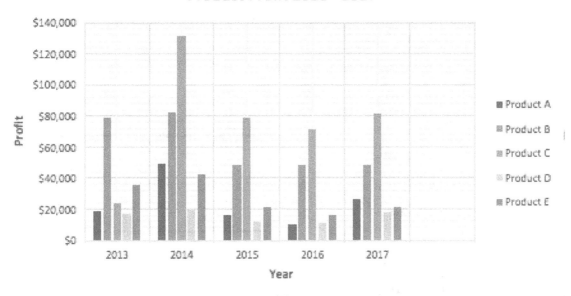

To Add Lines: Lines are not available for clustered column charts. However, in other chart types where you only compare two variables, you can add lines (e.g. target, average, reference, etc.) to your chart by checking the appropriate option.

To Add A Trendline:

- Click Add Chart Element and click Trendline. In addition to More Trendline Options, there are five options: None (default), Linear, Exponential, Linear Forecast, and Moving Average. Check the appropriate option for your data set. In this example, we will click Linear.

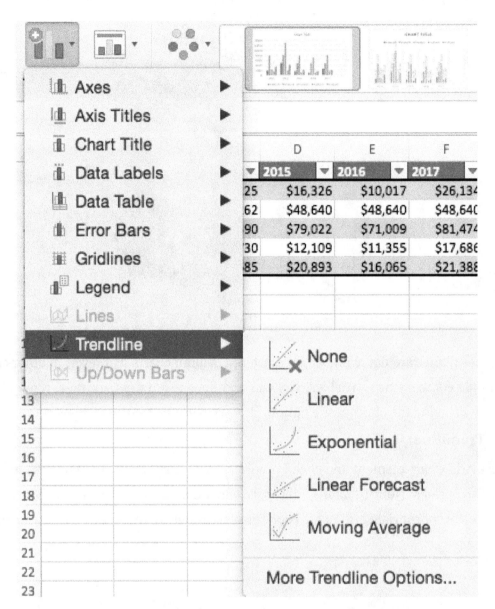

- Because we are comparing five different products over time, Excel creates a trendline for each product. To create a linear trendline for Product A, click Product A and click the blue OK button.

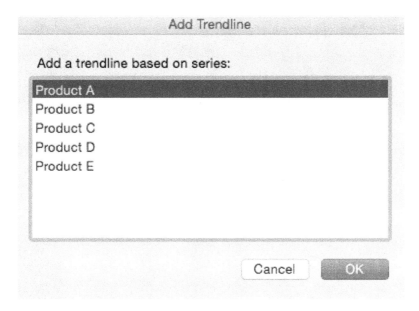

- The chart will now display a dotted trendline to represent the linear progression of Product A. Note that Excel has also added Linear (Product A) to the legend.

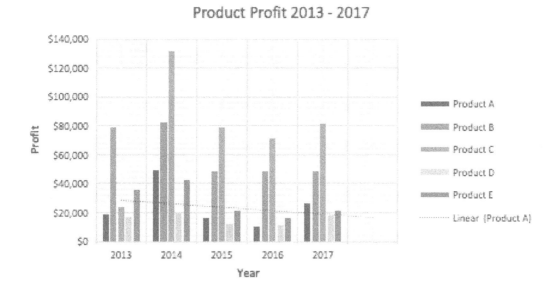

- To display the trendline equation on your chart, double click the trendline. A Format Trendline window will open on the right side of your screen. Click the box next to the Display equation on the chart at the bottom of the window. The equation now appears on your chart.

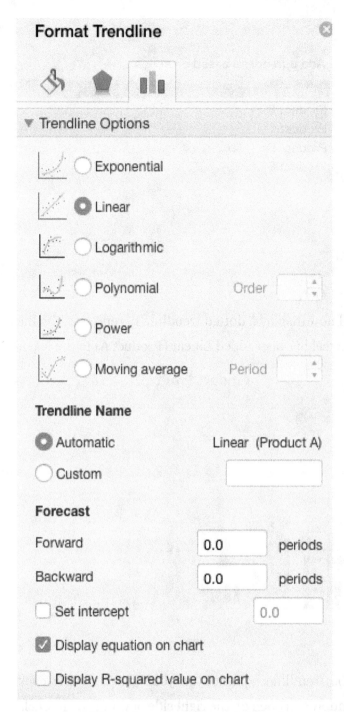

Note: You can create separate trendlines for as many variables in your chart as you like. For example, here is our chart with trendlines for Product A and Product C.

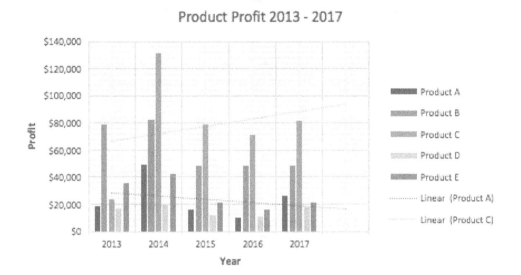

Product Profit 2013 - 2017

To Add Up/Down Bars: Up/Down Bars are not available for a column chart, but you can use them in a line chart to show increases and decreases among data points.

Step 4: Adjust Quick Layout

The second dropdown menu on the toolbar is Quick Layout, which allows you to quickly change the layout of elements in your chart (titles, legend, clusters, etc.).

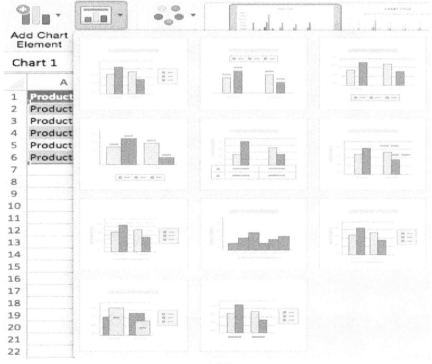

There are 11 quick layout options. Hover your cursor over the different options for an explanation and click the one you want to apply.

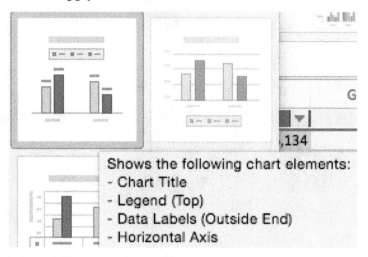

Step 5: Change Colors

The next dropdown menu in the toolbar is Change Colors. Click the icon and choose the color palette that fits your needs (these needs could be aesthetic, or match your brand's colors and style).

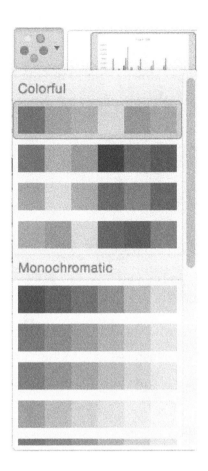

Step 6: Change Style

For cluster column charts, there are 14 chart styles available. Excel will default to Style 1, but you can select any of the other styles to change the chart appearance. Use the arrow on the right of the image bar to view other options.

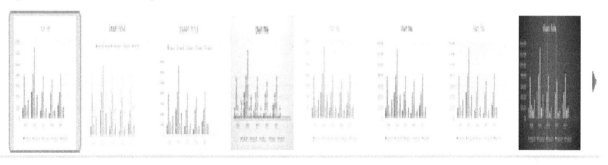

Step 7: Switch Row/Column

- Click the Switch Row/Column on the toolbar to flip the axes. Note: It is not always intuitive to flip axes for every chart, for example, if you have more than two variables.

- In this example, switching the row and column swaps the product and year (profit remains on the y-axis). The chart is now clustered by-product (not year), and the color-coded legend refers to the year (not product). To avoid confusion here, click on the legend and change the titles from Series to Years.

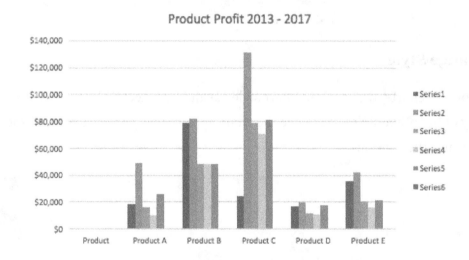

Step 8: Select Data

- Click the Select Data icon on the toolbar to change the range of your data.
- A window will open. Type the cell range you want and click the OK button. The chart will automatically update to reflect this new data range.

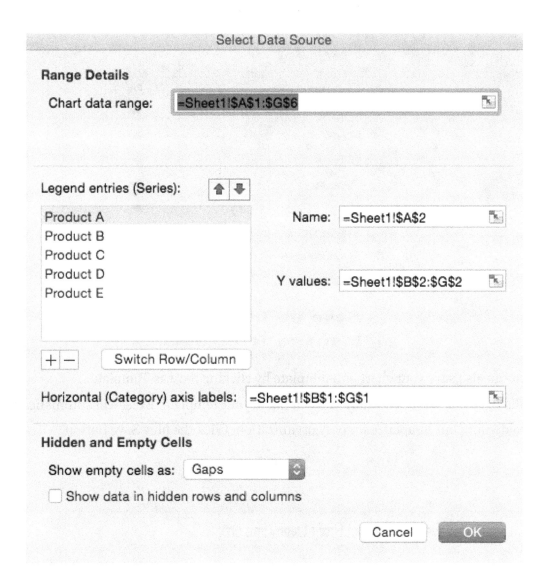

Select Data Source

Range Details

Chart data range: =Sheet1!$A$1:$G$6

Legend entries (Series):

Product A
Product B
Product C
Product D
Product E

Name: =Sheet1!$A$2

Y values: =Sheet1!$B$2:$G$2

\+ \− Switch Row/Column

Horizontal (Category) axis labels: =Sheet1!$B$1:$G$1

Hidden and Empty Cells

Show empty cells as: Gaps

☐ Show data in hidden rows and columns

Cancel   OK

Step 9: Change Chart Type

- Click the Change Chart Type dropdown menu.
- Here you can change your chart type to any of the nine chart categories that Excel offers. Of course, make sure that your data is appropriate for the chart type you choose.

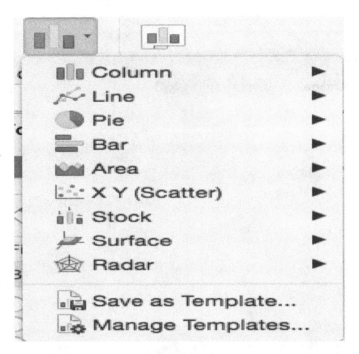

- You can also save your chart as a template by clicking Save as Template...
- A dialogue box will open where you can name your template. Excel will automatically create a folder for your templates for easy organization. Click the blue Save button.

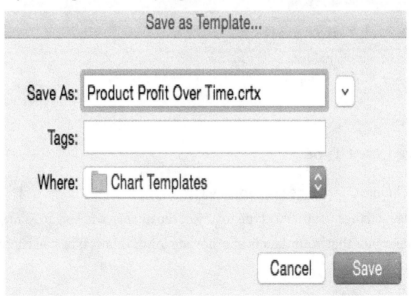

Step 10: Move Chart

- Click the Move Chart icon on the far right of the toolbar.

- A dialogue box appears where you can choose where to place your chart. You can either create a new sheet with this chart (New sheet) or place this chart as an object in another sheet (Object in). Click the blue OK button.

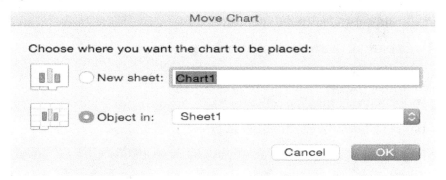

Step 11: Change Formatting

- The Format tab allows you to change the formatting of all elements and text in the chart, including colors, size, shape, fill, and alignment, and the ability to insert shapes. Click the Format tab and use the shortcuts available to create a chart that reflects your organization's brand (colors, images, etc.).
- Click the dropdown menu on the top left side of the toolbar and click the chart element you are editing.

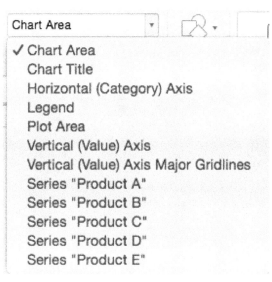

Step 12: Delete A Chart

- To delete a chart, simply click on it and click the Delete key on your keyboard.

How To Make A Graph In Excel

- Although graphs and charts are distinct, Excel groups all graphs under the chart's categories listed in the previous sections. To create a graph or another chart type, follow the steps below and select the appropriate graph type.

Select Range To Create A Graph From Workbook Data

- Highlight the cells that contain the data you want to use in your graph by clicking and dragging your mouse across the cells.
- Your cell range will now be highlighted in gray

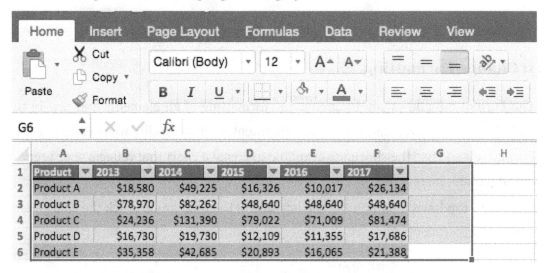

- Once the text is highlighted you can select a graph (which Excel refers to as a chart). Click the Insert tab and click Recommended Charts on the toolbar. Then click the type of graph you wish to use.

Now you have a graph. To customize your graph, you can follow the same steps explained in the previous section. All functionality for creating a chart remains the same when creating a graph.

How To Create A Table In Excel

If you don't need to make data visualization, you can also create a table in Excel using preexisting data. There are two ways to format a data set as a table:

1. Manually: In this example, we manually added data and formatted it as a table by including column and row names (products and years).

2. Use Excel's Format As Table Preset: You can also input raw data (numbers without any column and row names).

- To format data as a table, click and drag your mouse across the cells with the data range, click the Home tab, and click the Format as Table drop-down menu on the toolbar.

- Click New Table Style... (You will also see an option to use PivotTables. This feature is outside the scope of this how-to, but the concept is explained in the following section).

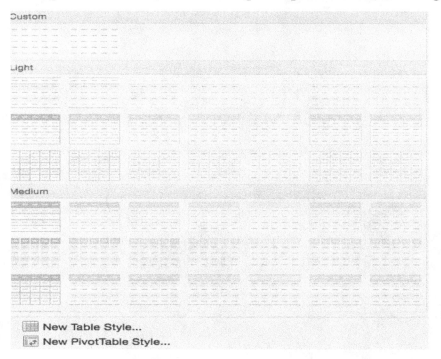

- A dialogue box opens and you can choose which aspects of the selected range to include in your formatted table. Click the blue OK button.

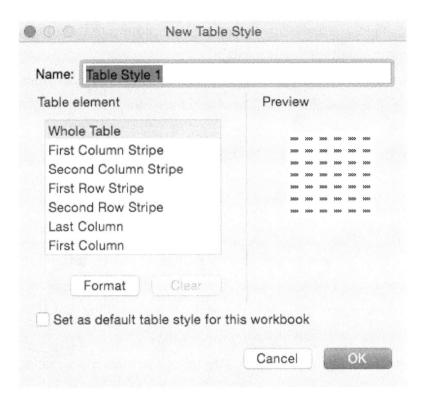

Top 5 Excel Chart And Graph Best Practices

Although Excel provides several layout and formatting presets to enhance the look and readability of your chart, using them won't ensure that you maximize the effectiveness of your chart. Below are the top five best practices to make your chart or graph as clear and useful as possible:

1. **Make It Clean:** Cluttered graphs with excessive colors or texts can be difficult to read and aren't eye-catching. Remove any unnecessary information so your audience can focus on the point you're trying to get across.

2. **Choose Appropriate Themes:** Consider your audience, the topic, and the main point of your chart when selecting a theme. While it can be fun to experiment with different styles, choose the theme that best fits your purpose.

3. **Use Text Wisely:** While charts and graphs are primarily visual tools, you will likely include some text (such as titles or axis labels). Be concise but use descriptive language, and be

intentional about the orientation of any text (for example, it's irritating to turn your head to read text written sideways on the x-axis).

4. **Place Elements Intelligently:** Pay attention to where you place titles, legends, symbols, and any other graphical elements. They should enhance your chart, not detract from it.

5. **Sort Data Before Creating The Chart:** People often forget to sort data or remove duplicates before creating the chart, which makes the visual unintuitive and can result in errors.

Data Visualization Tips

Now you know how to create graphs and charts in Excel. However, it is not the end of the story. Data visualization is not simply stacking several graphs together but is concerned with the ability to convey the correct message from the data to the reader in a compelling way. Here are some tips that will allow you to take your data visualization skills to a new level:

1. Keep It Simple: "Keep it simple" remains the golden rule in data visualization. Always try to make your graphs or charts as simple as possible. Remember that a reader should be able to understand the message that your chart intends to convey quickly.

2. Choose The Right Chart: Know the key differences between various types of charts such as bar, line, pie charts, etc. Learn about the advantages and disadvantages of each type of chart. This fundamental knowledge will ensure that you choose the most appropriate type of graph in your situation.

3. Pick The Right Colors: A color is a powerful tool in data visualization. Selecting the appropriate colors for a chart or graph may help your readers to grasp the key pieces of information quickly. When you use the right colors for a chart, remember that too similar colors cannot convey the differences between data points while extremely contrasting colors, as well as too many colors, can be distracting for a reader.

4. Properly Label Data: Data labeling is crucial to powerful data visualization. For example, it is always a good idea to label the axes of your chart and main data categories. Nevertheless, be aware that excessive labeling on your chart can be distracting to your readers.

5. Don't Use Special Effects: Don't use special effects (e.g., 3D) unless necessary. For example, a 3D feature on a bar chart is not necessary since a bar chart considers only two dimensions. Special effects may only distort dimensions on a chart, and a reader can be easily confused.

Related Excel Functionality

Excel is one of the most widely-used tools across any industry or type of organization. Charts and graphs are a great way to get started adding visualizations to your work, but there are several other ways to elevate your data in Excel. Below is a list of common features to create more "bang" with your data.

1. **Pivot Tables:** A pivot table allows you to extract certain columns or rows from a data set and reorganize or summarize that subset in a report. This is a useful tool if you only want to view a particular segment of a large data set, or if you want to view data from a new perspective.

2. **Conditional Formatting:** A powerful feature that allows you to apply specific formatting to certain cells in your spreadsheet. You can use conditional formatting to highlight key pieces of information, track changes, see deadlines, and perform many other data organization functions.

3. **Dashboards:** A powerful, visual reporting feature that pulls data from one or several datasets to display key performance indicators (KPIs), project or task status, and several other metrics. This gives the audience (team members, executives, clients, etc.) a snapshot view into project progress without surfacing private information.

4. **Collaborative Charts:** To avoid version control issues and allow multiple team members to edit a chart simultaneously, you'll want to use a collaborative chart tool. The desktop versions of Excel do not support this, but you can use Excel for Office 365, Microsoft's cloud-based web application, or several other online chart tools.

5. Data Series: A data series is any row or column stored in your workbook that you've slotted into a chart or graph. Once you've created your chart, you can add additional data series to it: Simply highlight the additional data you want to add and the chart will automatically update.

Make Better Decisions, Faster With Charts In Smartsheet

Empower your people to go above and beyond with a flexible platform designed to match the needs of your team and adapt as those needs change. The Smartsheet platform makes it easy to plan, capture, manage, and report on work from anywhere, helping your team be more effective and get more done. Report on key metrics and get real-time visibility into work as it happens with roll-up reports, dashboards, and automated workflows built to keep your team connected and informed. When teams have clarity into the work getting done, there's no telling how much more they can accomplish in the same amount of time.

CHAPTER 9: MERITS AND DEMERITS OF MICROSOFT EXCEL

Microsoft's Excel is the de facto standard for spreadsheet software and is an often indispensable tool for budgeting, financial forecasting, and data entry. Like any piece of software, however, Excel isn't perfect. Before you invest in a license, compare the pros and cons to decide whether Excel is right for you.

From basic accounting to data management, MS Excel has indefinite uses. So if you are about to invest in an MS Office suite to scale up your accounting skills, it's a good move to make. However, considering the Advantages and Disadvantages of MS Excel for business is what you need for accounting specifically.

Microsoft Excel, widely known as MS-Excel or just Excel, is a very versatile application software developed by Microsoft. This tool is used by around 90% of small and large-scale companies around the world.

MS Excel is available for Windows, Android, macOS, and iOS. It is often used to calculate data and for tasks that involve graphing information because it comes as part of the Microsoft Office Suite. Those who have used this tool before know that this is one of the most powerful applications from Microsoft so far.

Microsoft Excel is a powerful spreadsheet program that has been around since 1985. It's now the most popular spreadsheet software globally, with over 1600 million copies sold as of April 2016. With the world being more data-driven than ever, Microsoft Excel is one of the products that offer the tools to analyze that data differently. And while they can always limit themselves, it's worth noting that all this information is not limited to rows and columns amounting up to 100. It goes into the thousands.

But it's not without its flaws; it's time to identify some of the pros and cons of using MS excel for your business. However, it can be a bit difficult to understand for those who are new to it at first.

Advantages Of Microsoft Excel

Microsoft Excel allows you to manipulate, manage and analyze data, helping assist in decision-making and creating efficiencies that will directly affect your bottom line. Whether you're using it for business or to help manage personal databases and expenses, Microsoft Excel gives you the right tools to enable you to accomplish all your needs. Whether you're a student, business professional, or an amateur spreadsheet maker, Microsoft Excel is the go-to tool for all sorts of data analysis.

From basic arithmetic to complex formulas and calculations, it can do just about anything you need your spreadsheets to accomplish.

As a result, there are more reasons than ever before to make Excel your one-stop solution for everything related to numbers on a screen. If you are a newbie, here are some advantages of MS Excel to check out on your way to working with rows and columns.

The advantages of Excel are wide and varied; here are the main advantages:

1. Easy And Effective Comparisons: With the powerful analytical tools included within Microsoft Excel, you can analyze large amounts of data to discover trends and patterns that will influence decisions. Microsoft Excel's graphing capabilities allow you to summarize your data, enhancing your ability to organize and structure your data.

2. Macros And Templates: One of the advantages of MS Excel is that it has templates and macros. Macros allow a user to automate repetitive tasks to save time, while templates are preprogrammed files with placeholder data for easy use. A few common examples include:

- Budgeting spreadsheets to prepare budgets by company division or department.
- Expense report template for organizing receipts from trips or work meetings.
- Vacation planner spreadsheet with tabs for months and days and notes sections for travel plans, packing lists, activities, etc.
- Client prospect lists can be used when meeting new clients who may not have heard about your services yet.

3. Formulas Are A Great Advantage Of MS Excel: This software comes with various formulas and calculation features that make bookkeeping very easy for accounting professionals. For example, it's easier to calculate things like loans, time-related data such as days until the holidays or weeks left in the school year; statistics for sampling purposes such as average monthly expenses or budgeting numbers based on historical data; profit margins by using cost per unit (CPU) versus selling price per unit (SPU).

4. Powerful Analysis Of Large Amounts Of Data: Recent upgrades to the Excel spreadsheet enhance your ability to analyze large amounts of data. With powerful filtering, sorting, and search tools, you can quickly and easily narrow down the criteria that will assist in your decisions. Combine these tools with the tables, pivot tables, and graphs, and you can find the information that you want quickly and easily, even if you have hundreds of thousands of data items. While you will need the latest technology to get the best out of Microsoft Excel, it is scalable and can be used at home on your low-powered PC or at work on your high-powered Laptop.

5. Working Together: With the advent of the Excel Web App, you can now work on spreadsheets simultaneously with other users. The ability to work together enhances your ability to streamline processes and allows for 'brainstorming' sessions with large sets of data, the collaboration tools allow you to get the most out of the sharing capabilities of Microsoft Excel. The bonus is that as the Excel Worksheet is web-based, you can collaborate anywhere, you are no longer tied to your desk but can work on spreadsheets on the go, this is ideal for a businessman on the go.

6. Microsoft Excel Mobile & iPad Apps: With the advent of the tablet and the smartphone, it is now possible to take your worksheets to a client or a meeting without having to bring along your Laptop. The power of these mobile devices now allows you to manipulate data and update your spreadsheets, and then view the spreadsheets immediately on your phone or tablet.

Disadvantages Of Microsoft Excel

Microsoft Excel is an excellent program for creating spreadsheets and graphs. It's a powerful tool, but it has its limitations too. Most of the problems with MS Excel are related to accounting. That's why many professionals prefer using advanced accounting tools such as Xero, Freshbooks, or Quickbooks. You may also have to deal with the following disadvantages of MS Excel if you have mastered it.

1. Not Easy To Share: Microsoft has made great strides with their Web applications, but the sharing functionality still has a long way to go to become world-class. Part of the problem is that often the ability for sharing a tool requires extra software to be installed on the PC, and this often becomes cumbersome. Tools like Google Documents are revolutionizing the way people share documents online.

2. Nonrelational: I use MS Access for databases and love the relational aspect of the database. The idea that you can link data by common elements (such as employee ID, Stock Number, etc.) greatly assists in the reduction of data and the ability to analyze data. Aside from some database functions and some lookup tools, Microsoft Excel lacks any true relational functionality.

3. Scalability: Excel 2010 has introduced larger spreadsheets and binary formats; however, using large amounts of data on the average PC will slow down and often freeze the PC. As some of the competing tools are in the 'cloud' file size does not become a problem.

4. No Forms: while you can use forms within VBA, the average user will not have much knowledge of VBA and therefore not be able to incorporate functional forms into their spreadsheets quickly.

5. Customizable Graphs: Microsoft Excel does offer a good variety of graph capabilities; however, the customization of the standard formats and the combination of different data sets and different types of graphs is awkward and not intuitive. For a powerful worksheet, this is a big disadvantage.

6. Data And Growth: One of the main problems with MS Excel is that it can't handle more than a few thousand rows without slowing to a crawl. It also imposes limitations on file size. But there are ways around this, just as there are solutions for any issue of an app or software tool. The key thing is not to give up if you find yourself in one of these situations; instead, look at the tools available in Excel and use them creatively to have their intended effect.

7. Difficult To Learn: Another Limitation of MS Excel is that it can be difficult to learn. This is because there are many different elements, such as formulas, functions, and keyboard shortcuts. However, this disadvantage may be alleviated with Excel tutorials for beginners or using templates to start quickly with a good learning method and regular practice.

8. Difficult Formulas Are A Major Disadvantage Of MS Excel: This disadvantage is that there are different levels of difficulty when using MS Excel. For example, some people may be more comfortable with the idea of completing a quick task such as creating an inventory list for customers to replenish their shelves, while others may not know how to write formulas and create charts which could take up valuable time. You need to be well-versed with formulas properly and the syntax to avoid any errors.

9. No Quick Autofill Features: One more problem with this software is that there are no quick autofill features. Lack of knowledge of how formulas work can be another painful experience for someone with basic knowledge.

Therefore, you'd require learning from within the interface itself; however, these disadvantages can also provide an opportunity for continued personal growth and development outside of just mastery over MS EXCEL skillset.

10. Calculation Errors: The most problematic of the disadvantages of MS Excel is that there are errors in calculations. For example, when working with fractions or percentages, the decimal point may be misplaced, and it would cause an error to appear on the screen.

This can make it difficult for someone who does not know what they are doing to fix this problem without assistance from an expert. Also, you'll have to know using the date and currency formats properly.

The Advantages & Disadvantages Of Spreadsheets

In business, strategic planning is essential and requires valid information to make key decisions. Choosing the right tools for inputting, tracking, analyzing, and storing data will help business owners and managers make the best choices for their company's business. One of the components within software productivity suites is the spreadsheet. Spreadsheets are popular among accountants and among those who like to collect and track data, yet there are some limitations, which may not make them the best choice for every office application.

Advantage: Organizing Data

Spreadsheets are frequently the go-to tool for collecting and organizing data, which is among the simplest of its uses. Information can easily be placed in neat columns and rows and then sorted by information type. Although a large collection of data may be overwhelming to view in its raw state, tools within the program allow the user to create presentations where the data is analyzed and plugged into pie charts or tables for easy viewing and interpretation.

Disadvantage: User Bias

However, the downside is that only the information that the user chooses for analysis is included in these presentations, and therefore, other pertinent information that may influence decision making might be excluded, unintentionally. To make reporting of data more user-friendly and comprehensive, companies are choosing to use reporting tools such as Tableau and Qlik, instead of relying solely on the spreadsheet.

Advantage: Streamlines Calculations

No one likes to spend all their time at work doing repetitive calculations. The great appeal of spreadsheets is that the program does all the math for the user. Once a formula is written and the program has a set command, complex calculations can easily be computed for the related data that has been input. This allows users to ask "what if" types of questions and to easily get the answers they need without the need to rework the calculations.

For example, if the spreadsheet is set up to calculate your gross profit when any variable such as cost per unit, shipping costs, or sales discount is changed, the software automatically recalculates the new gross profit based on the new information.

Disadvantage: Learning The Syntax Takes Skill

The difficult part for many users is that the calculations must be entered into the spreadsheet as formulas. This requires learning the correct syntax for each type of calculation you wish to make. Although many classes are available to learn the skills necessary to use these formulas, many users still find them difficult. If the syntax is incorrect, the program will not return the correct information when the calculations are run. Additionally, if users input the wrong data, even in only one cell of the spreadsheet, all related calculations and cells will be affected and have incorrect data.

Advantage: Multiple User Access

In today's collaborative work environment, multiple users within an office often need access to the same documents. If using Microsoft Excel, the spreadsheets can be shared, but only one user can change data at a time. If local copies are made and updated, other users will not have access to the new data. Google Sheets offers the solution of file sharing and allowing multiple users to access and update a single form. Be aware that, in both cases, there is no file history. Therefore, no matter who makes changes at any time, when any changes are made, the previous information history is lost.

Disadvantage: Lack Of Security

Another spreadsheet disadvantage is the lack of security for your files. Typically, spreadsheets are not that secure and therefore are at greater risk for data corruption or mismanagement of information. Files that contain sensitive financial information may not be safe from hackers, even if password protected.

Other types of data collection software therefore may be a more suitable option. Access, Oracle, or some other form of the relational database has built-in safeguards that protect data integrity and prevent the reorganization of information. For example, in a spreadsheet, a user might sort a column of information and may inadvertently cause-related information, such as first and last name, to become out of sync. In contrast, a database will keep all parts of a record unified, thereby ensuring better data integrity.

Why Sheets Might Be A Better Option For You

Now that we have addressed both the advantages and disadvantages of Microsoft Excel, let us look at why using Google Sheets might be a better option for you and/or your business.

For starters, Google Sheets is a mobile-first platform. What that means is you do not have to have a power-hungry desktop or laptop to leverage Sheets at your business. Sheets will run on almost any device including outdated smartphones, and the mobile app is great.

Since Google Sheets is a mobile-first platform, it can be accessed from any device that has an internet connection and a compatible browser. As such, you could still have access to your documents through the Google Drive platform from a computer at a public library, a hotel, or from someone else's phone.

Taking it a step further, the mobile-first platform also gives you the ability to share your documents with others without having to save and send them. Instead, you simply send them a link to your document and allow them to look through it. And yet, Sheets goes beyond simply sharing. Not only can you share your documents, but you can also do real-time collaboration and/or editing with users who have access to your link. This is not possible with Microsoft Excel unless you have an active subscription to Office 365 (which is costly).

So, is it possible that sheets could be better?

Let's recap:

- It is a mobile-first software suite.
- It does not require expensive computers to run.
- Accessible from any device with an internet connection.
- Simplified sharing.
- Real-time collaboration and/or editing.
- It sure looks like it might be...

Which One Is Best For Business Users?

So, here is where things get a little tricky...

In most cases, Google Sheets is neck-and-neck with Microsoft Excel.

- Both have the same formulas.
- Both can create customized formulas.

216

- Both can create colorful layouts and sheets.
- Both can be saved in multiple formats.

And recently, Google added the ability to use macros; a feature that Excel rocked while Sheets slept.

Where They Are Different Is Why It Gets Tricky.

If you are an advanced user who has ultra-complex formulas, deep-level computations, or a ton of recurring formulas across multiple forms, Excel is your best option. But, if you are the average user (most likely the case; there are better solutions besides Sheets or Excel for the prior user), then Sheets will work just as well as Excel, it's lighter-weight, snappier, and has enhanced collaboration capabilities. Because sheets are simple, clean, free to use, and allow for sharing and real-time collaboration, it wins the battle for us, and for an increasing number of business users who are switching to G Suite from Microsoft Office. While Office 365 offers most of the same tools to businesses, it can't compete with the pricing model offered by Google in G Suite.

What Can Microsoft Excel Be Used For?

Microsoft Excel is a very versatile tool and can be used for almost anything that you can imagine:

- Agendas
- Budgets
- Calendars
- Cards
- Charts and diagrams
- Financial tools (loan calculators, etc.)
- Flyers
- Forms
- Inventories
- Invoices
- Lists and to-do checklists
- Planners
- Plans and proposals
- Reports
- Schedules
- Timesheets

This is a small selection of what can be achieved on Microsoft Excel.

CHAPTER 10: BENEFITS OF MICROSOFT EXCEL

The Benefits of Using Microsoft Excel

Excel is a powerful tool for building bespoke template-based spreadsheets for use in business, for analysis of data, and for presenting data graphically. We have helped many clients use it in their business to great effect, but here are the benefits of Excel according to Microsoft:

- MS Excel features the Microsoft Office Fluent user interface to help you find powerful tools when you need them.
- Find the tools you want when you need them using the results-oriented Office Fluent user interface. Based on the job you need to accomplish, whether it's creating a table or writing a formula, the new versions present the appropriate commands when you need them.
- Import, Organize and explore massive data sets within significantly expanded spreadsheets.
- Work with massive amounts of data, which supports spreadsheets that can be up to 1 million rows by 16,000 columns. In addition to the bigger grid, Excel supports multicore processor platforms for faster calculation of formula-intense spreadsheets.
- Use the completely redesigned charting engine to communicate your analysis in professional-looking charts.
- Build professional-looking charts faster with fewer clicks using charting tools in the Office Fluent user interface. Apply rich visual enhancements to your charts such as 3-D effects, soft shadowing, and transparency. Create and interact with charts the same way, regardless of the application you are using, because the charting engine is consistent in Microsoft Office Word and Microsoft Office PowerPoint.
- Enjoy improved and powerful support for working with tables.
- Create, format, expand, filter, and refer to tables within formulas because the support for tables has been greatly improved. When you're viewing data contained in a large table, Excel keeps table headings in view while you scroll.
- Create and work with interactive PivotTable views with ease.
- PivotTable views enable you to quickly reorient your data to help you answer multiple questions. Find the answers you need faster and create and use PivotTable views more easily by dragging fields where you want them to be displayed.

- "See" important trends and find exceptions in your data.

- Apply conditional formatting to your information more easily to discover patterns and highlight trends in your data. New schemes include color gradients, heat maps, data bars, and performance indicator icons.

- Use Microsoft Excel on your desktop and online to help share spreadsheets more securely with others.

- Using Excel 365 online you can share spreadsheets so others can access the information using a web browser. Users can navigate, sort, filter, input parameters, and interact with the information, all within their web browser and all sharing the same file so that updates from anyone are reflected for all.

- Help ensure you and your organization work with the most current business information.

- Prevent the spread of multiple or outdated copies of a spreadsheet throughout your organization by using Excel 365 online. Control which users can view and modify spreadsheets on the server using permission-based access.

- Reduce the size of spreadsheets and improve damaged file recovery at the same time.

- The new, compressed Microsoft Office Excel XML Format offers a dramatic reduction in file size, while its architecture offers an improvement in data recovery for damaged files. This new format provides a tremendous saving to storage and bandwidth requirements and reduces the burden on IT personnel.

- Extend your business intelligence investments because Excel provides full support for Microsoft SQL Server.

- Take advantage of the flexibility and the new cube functions to build a custom report from an OLAP database. You can also connect to external sources of data more easily using the Data Connection Library.

Business Benefits of Advanced Microsoft Excel

All companies need to evolve and push forward to stay competitive in today's world. One way to lead the pack and promote profitability is by implementing development programs so that employees can continue to stay on top of the latest technologies and work as efficiently as possible. Continual training and advancement can also enable employers to protect one of their most valuable assets: their workforce.

Talented employees want to be challenged and strive hard to stay at the head of the pack. By providing them with the continuing education they need to be as effective as they wish to be, employers can improve retention, lowering employee turnover, as well the risk of losing the most talented staff members to competitors. One program often included in these education training programs is Excel for Business.

What is Excel used for? Excel provides users with the ability to calculate, organize, and evaluate quantitative data, allowing managers and senior staff to have the information they need to make important decisions that can affect the company. By having employees trained in the advanced functions of Excel, they can better present their information up to upper management. It is also a critical skill for employees hoping to climb to the top themselves.

There are benefits to learning advanced Excel for both employees and employers alike. Let's take a deeper look at the advantages of Excel when companies include it as part of their routine employee training.

Benefits of Excel For Employees

Employees can benefit from advanced Excel training in many ways, from increasing value to learning better tools to improve their work output.

1. Sharpening Your Skill Set

Continuing to learn and hone your skillset is crucial to advancing your career. Advanced Excel training focuses on several critical skills that can be utilized and valued in almost any position in a company. After training, you should be better able to:

- Visualize, manipulate, and evaluate the data.
- Create equations that can allow you to provide more data on vital company functions, such as workflow, project efficiency, financial projections and budgets, and even inventory levels and usage.
- Create an easy-to-read set of data that can be used by upper management to analyze current projects or situations in the company.
- Design spreadsheets that better organize data and provide a better picture of the information that is input.
- Read and comprehend spreadsheets and data from other departments, vendors, and customers.

- Provide answers and solutions to problems affecting the business by being able to interpret data at a more advanced level.

- Maintain, organize, and balance complex financial and inventory accounts.

- Create tracking systems for different departments and operations, including various workflow processes.

Advanced Microsoft Excel training will not only provide employers with higher-skilled employees but will also provide employees with tools that can help them work more effectively in their current positions and equip them to advance to higher-level positions.

2. Improving Your Efficiency And Productivity

Excel is a vital tool for speeding up productivity and allowing workers to be more efficient when dealing with large amounts of data and calculations. When you understand Excel at a more advanced level, you will have the ability to use its more sophisticated tools, which will allow you to complete your tasks and analyze your data more quickly. It will also allow you to keep team members up-to-date on data, which can streamline the workflow process.

Even better, knowing advanced Excel will allow you to better streamline your calculations. Repetitive calculations take time, especially when you have to double-check your work. With advanced Excel tools, you can create more complex calculations. Once your formula is written and you have programmed your set command, the program will perform all of the work to complete the calculations, freeing up your time for other tasks and ensuring that you have accurate data the first time around.

3. Making Yourself A More Valuable Member Of The Company

Being a valuable employee not only will provide you with better job security, but also opens up opportunities for advancement. The way to make yourself vital to the company is by being more efficient, better educated, and better skilled in your job functions. That is what training in advanced Excel can provide you. Employees should always find ways to increase their value to the company to avoid becoming replaceable by newer workers with a more advanced skill set. Learning and mastering new skills is crucial to stay on top of your game and set yourself up for greater security and advancement.

4. Making You Better At Organizing Data

A common go-to tool for collecting and organizing data in spreadsheets. And, in its simplest form, Excel is spreadsheet software. It allows you to carefully organize all of your data while providing you with the ability to sort the information in any way that you choose. Data in a raw state can be overwhelming and hard to analyze. With the advanced capabilities of Excel, you will be able to organize your information better, make calculations when necessary, and sort the information so that it can be appropriately analyzed and transferred to graphs or charts for better viewing.

5. It Can Make Your Job Easier

The more proficient at Excel you become, the more quickly you will be able to navigate the system. Microsoft Excel features several shortcuts that can enable you to work faster and even learn more complicated Excel strategies that can be used across the entire suite of Microsoft Office products. You also will be able to use the data in your Excel sheet across a variety of programs, reducing your need to re-enter information and allowing you to streamline your workflow better. The easier your job is, and the better equipped you are to handle it, the more likely you are to enjoy your work. There have been studies that show happier workers are 20% more productive than their unhappy counterparts. The easier your work is, the happier and more productive of an employee you will be.

Advantages of Advanced Excel For Employers

Not only can advanced Excel training and knowledge provide added benefits for your employees, but it can also provide numerous benefits for the company.

1. It Creates Greater Efficiency And Heightens Productivity

Yes, advanced training in Microsoft Excel can improve the efficiency and productivity of employees, as mentioned above, which will translate into greater efficiency and heightened productivity for the company. The more efficient your employee's work, the quicker tasks, and projects will get done, allowing you to provide your customers and clients with better service and allowing more work to be output in a shorter period. Even if the benefits of advanced Excel training shave a half-hour off of your employee's time, when multiplied by the number of employees in the entire department or company, it can translate into a significant amount of extra staff hours per week for other work.

2. It Allows You To Better Use An Asset You Have Already Acquired

Your software programs are assets of your company and ones that can be considered underutilized if the employees are not trained to maximize their use. Continued training on the tools and facets of Excel will allow you to get the most out of that asset as well as other assets that may not have been used to their maximum efficiency, such as inventory management systems. For example, if your employees can better streamline calculations and organize data, you can improve inventory management, making better use of those assets as well.

3. It Allows You To Grow Employee Knowledge With Little Expense And Effort

The employees in your company are already trained in the original Excel program, and implementing simple training programs that allow you to better use the program can be significantly less expensive than having to train new hires, who already know these advanced systems, in your company's processes and procedures. Additionally, advanced training can be easy, usually taking a couple of weeks or less for employees who are already proficient at a more intermediate level. You also can save money by hiring an onsite trainer who can train a large portion of your workforce at once, instead of investing in outside training programs for each employee to take. It translates into a more educated and skilled staff at a minimal cost.

4. It Takes Stress Off Of Your IT Support Team

When employees are not appropriately trained in all aspects of a software program, it can fall to your IT department to pick up the slack. Having IT staffers move workstation-to-workstation to train co-workers individually prevents them from focusing on more productive tasks, such as system upgrades, maintaining security, and hardware installs and maintenance.

Additionally, just because your IT department can help employees with the use of the software, it does not mean they are using it to its greatest capacity and producing the needed data and information needed for the products. Their talents lie with the technical side, and they may not understand the use or function of the information they are helping the employee to produce. If your employees are trained in advanced Excel, they will be able to handle their data manipulations, saving the time they would normally wait on IT and producing better results.

5. It Can Help Your Talent Retention Efforts And Provide Employees With A More Satisfactory Job Experience

Valuable employees thrive learning new skills that can help them not only excel in their current position but also move up the ranks. Failing to feed this need to learn can lower your employee's happiness with their job and diminish their motivation to continue their career path with their current company. When you educate employees, you make them more valuable to the company, while reducing turnover and providing your most talented employees with a reason to stick around.

Thorough employee training is a critical component of advancing your workforce, improving productivity, and retaining a solid employee base. Whether you choose to invest in onsite training

223

to bring your employees up-to-date on advanced Excel operation or enable them to pursue outside training opportunities, such as a master's program featuring Advanced Excel coursework, continuing education for your employees is essential to continue to grow your company and stay ahead of competitors in your industry.

As they say, knowledge is power, and there is no better way to empower your workforce, improve their skills, and make them more valuable to the company than allowing them to use vital programs to maximum effectiveness. Keep your employees motivated, keep them learning, and keep them producing efficiently by using advanced Excel training to improve their day-to-day work.

CHAPTER 11: MICROSOFT EXCEL SHORTCUTS AND TIPS

There's no denying the fact that shortcuts make our lives easier and if you're a Microsoft Excel user, you can refer to this guide to learn some of the major ones. You might be surprised to learn about the variety of Excel shortcuts that are there, and while we do not expect you to remember all of them, it is always good to have a list that is just a glance away. Read on, as we list some of the most important Microsoft Excel shortcuts for Windows to make your work easier.

Microsoft Excel Keyboard Shortcuts

Before you proceed, note that the list is pretty long but it is by no means a complete list consisting of all the Excel shortcuts. However, we have picked out some of the most useful shortcuts, and we hope this would be worth your time.

1. Ctrl + N: To create a new workbook.

2. Ctrl + O: To open a saved workbook.

3. Ctrl + S: To save a workbook.

4. Ctrl + A: To select all the contents in a workbook.

5. Ctrl + B: To turn highlighted cells bold.

6. Ctrl + C: To copy cells that are highlighted.

7. Ctrl + D: To fill the selected cell with the content of the cell right above.

8. Ctrl + F: To search for anything in a workbook.

9. Ctrl + G: To jump to a certain area with a single command.

10. Ctrl + H: To find and replace cell contents.

11. Ctrl + I: To italicize cell contents.

12. Ctrl + K: To insert a hyperlink in a cell.

13. Ctrl + L: To open the create table dialog box.

14. Ctrl + P: To print a workbook.

15. Ctrl + R: To fill the selected cell with the content of the cell on the left.

16. Ctrl + U: To underline highlighted cells.

17. Ctrl + V: To paste anything that was copied.

18. Ctrl + W: To close your current workbook.

19. Ctrl + Z: To undo the last action.

20. Ctrl + 1: To format the cell contents.

21. Ctrl + 5: To put a strikethrough in a cell.

22. Ctrl + 8: To show the outline symbols.

23. Ctrl + 9: To hide a row.

24. Ctrl + 0: To hide a column.

25. Ctrl + Shift + :: To enter the current time in a cell.

26. Ctrl +: To enter the current date in a cell.

27. Ctrl + `: To change the view from displaying cell values to formulas.

28. Ctrl + ': To copy the formula from the cell above.

29. Ctrl + -: To delete columns or rows.

30. Ctrl + Shift + =: To insert columns and rows.

31. Ctrl + Shift + ~: To switch between displaying Excel formulas or their values in the cell.

32. Ctrl + Shift + @: To apply time formatting.

33. Ctrl + Shift + !: To apply comma formatting.

34. Ctrl + Shift + $: To apply currency formatting.

35. Ctrl + Shift + #: To apply date formatting.

36. Ctrl + Shift + %: To apply percentage formatting.

37. Ctrl + Shift + &: To place borders around the selected cells.

38. Ctrl + Shift + _: To remove a border.

39. Ctrl + -: To delete a selected row or column.

40. Ctrl + Spacebar: To select an entire column.

41. Ctrl + Shift + Spacebar: To select an entire workbook.

42. Ctrl + Home: To redirect to cell A1.

43. Ctrl + Shift + Tab: To switch to the previous workbook.

44. Ctrl + Shift + F: To open the fonts menu under format cells.

45. Ctrl + Shift + O: To select the cells containing comments.

46. Ctrl + Drag: To drag and copy a cell or to a duplicate worksheet.

47. Ctrl + Shift + Drag: To drag and insert copy.

48. Ctrl + Up arrow: To go to the topmost cell in a current column.

49. Ctrl + Down arrow: To jump to the last cell in a current column.

50. Ctrl + Right arrow: To go to the last cell in a selected row.

51. Ctrl + Left arrow: To jump back to the first cell in a selected row.

52. Ctrl + End: To go to the last cell in a workbook.

53. Alt + Page down: To move the screen towards the right.

54. Alt + Page Up To move the screen towards the left.

55. Ctrl + F2: To open the print preview window.

56. Ctrl + F1: To expand or collapse the ribbon.

57. Alt: To open the access keys.

58. Tab: Move to the next cell.

59. Alt + F + T: To open the options.

60. Alt + Down arrow: To activate filters for cells.

61. F2: To edit a cell.

62. F3: To paste a cell name if the cells have been named.

63. Shift + F2: To add or edit a cell comment.

64. Alt + H + H: To select a fill color.

65. Alt + H + B: To add a border.

66. Ctrl + 9: To hide the selected rows.

67. Ctrl + 0: To hide the selected columns.

68. Esc: To cancel an entry.

69. Enter: To complete the entry in a cell and move to the next one.

70. Shift + Right arrow: To extend the cell selection to the right.

71. Shift + Left arrow: To extend the cell selection to the left.

72. Shift + Space: To select the entire row.

73. Page up/ down: To move the screen up or down.

74. Alt + H: To go to the Home tab in Ribbon.

75. Alt + N: To go to the Insert tab in Ribbon.

76. Alt + P: To go to the Page Layout tab in Ribbon.

77. Alt + M: To go to the Formulas tab in Ribbon.

78. Alt + A: To go to the Data tab in Ribbon.

79. Alt + R: To go to the Review tab in Ribbon.

80. Alt + W: To go to the View tab in Ribbon.

81. Alt + Y: To open the Help tab in Ribbon.

82. Alt + Q: To quickly jump to search.

83. Alt + Enter: To start a new line in a current cell.

84. Shift + F3: To open the Insert function dialog box.

85. F9: To calculate workbooks.

86. Shift + F9: To calculate an active workbook.

87. Ctrl + Alt + F9: To force calculate all workbooks.

88. Ctrl + F3: To open the name manager.

89. Ctrl + Shift + F3: To create names from values in rows and columns.

90. Ctrl + Alt + +: To zoom in inside a workbook.

91. Ctrl + Alt +: To zoom out inside a workbook.

92. Alt + 1: To turn on Autosave.

93. Alt + 2: To save a workbook.

94. Alt + F + E: To export your workbook.

95. Alt + F + Z: To share your workbook.

96. Alt + F + C: To close and save your workbook.

97. Alt or F11: To turn key tips on or off.

98. Alt + Y + W: To know what's new in Microsoft Excel.

99. F1: To open Microsoft Excel help.

100. Ctrl + F4: To close Microsoft Excel.

Excel Tips For Becoming A Spreadsheet Pro

1. Paint Cells To A New Format

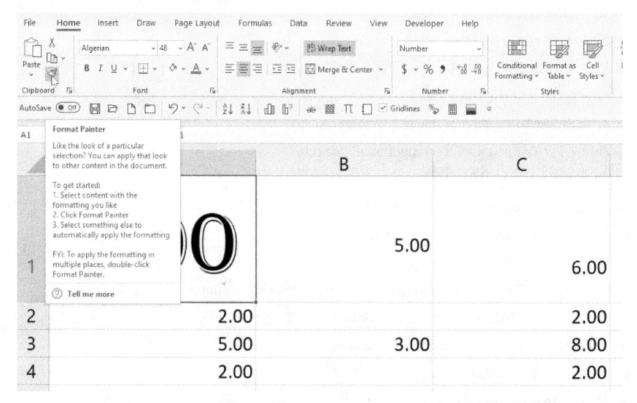

Let's say you change not only the wrapping in a cell but also the entire look—the font, the color, whatever. And you want to apply it to many, many other cells. The trick is the Format Painter tool, the one that is on the Home tab that looks like a paintbrush.

Select the sell you like, click the icon, and then click on a different cell to paint in the format—they'll match in looks, not in content. Want to apply it to multiple tabs? Double-click the paintbrush icon, then click away on multiple cells.

2. Line Breaks And Wrapping Text

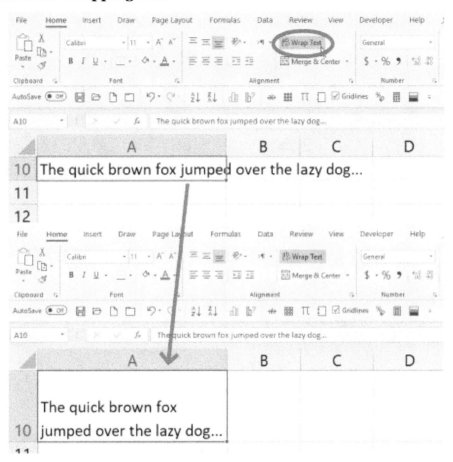

Typing into spreadsheet cells can be frustrating, as the default for the text you type is to continue forever, without wrapping back down to a new line. You can change that. Create a new line by typing Alt+Enter (hitting Enter alone takes you out of the cell). Or, click the Wrap Text option under the Home tab at the top of the screen, which means all text wraps right at the edge of the cell you're in. Resize the row/column and the text re-wraps to fit.

If you've got multiple cells that have text overruns, select them all before you click Wrap Text. Or, select all the cells before you even type in them and click Wrap Text. Then whatever you type will wrap in the future.

3. AutoFill Your Cells

	A	B	C	D	E	F
				D2	9:00:00 AM	
1	Numbers	Formula	Names \ Text	Time	Dates	Days of the week
2	1	2.5	Bob	9:00 AM	1/1/2013	Monday
3	2	3.5	William		Copy Cells	
4	3	4.5	Susan		Fill Series	
5	4	5.5	Bob		Fill Formatting Only	
6	5	6.5	William		Fill Without Formatting	
7	6	7.5	Susan		Fill Days	
8	7	8.5	Bob		Fill Weekdays	
9	8	9.5	William		Fill Months	
10	9	10.5	Susan		Fill Years	
11					Linear Trend	
					Growth Trend	
					Flash Fill	
					Series...	

Intro | AutoFill - All Directions | **AutoFill - Copy and Fill** | Flash Fill - Numbers | Flash Fill - Text | ⊕

This is a no-brainer, but so easily overlooked. You start typing a series of repetitive things like dates (1/1/20, 1/2/20, 1/3/20, etc.) and you know you're in for a long day. Instead, begin the series and move the cursor on the screen to the lower-right part of the last cell, the fill handle. When it turns into a plus sign (+), click and drag down to select all the cells you need to fill. They'll magically fill using the pattern you started. It can also go up a column, or left or right on a row.

Even better you can AutoFill without much of a pattern. Again, pick a cell or cells, move to the fill handle, right-click, and drag. You'll get a menu of options. The more data you input at first, the better the Fill Series option will do creating your AutoFill options.

4. Flash Fill, Fastest Fill Alive

F3   Luke Loya

	A	B	C	D	E	F
1	Dates		Last Name	Middle Name	First Name	Name
2	1/1/2013		hatley	william	michael	Michael Hatley
3	1/2/2013		loya	a	luke	Luke Loya
4	1/3/2013		clegg		jerome	Jerome Clegg
5	1/4/2013		Rinaldi	bruce	alvin	Alvin Rinaldi
6	1/5/2013		Lawrence	c	sue	Sue Lawrence
7	1/6/2013		surratt		Jean	Jean Surratt
8	1/7/2013		rulkey	jim	doug	Doug Rulkey
9	1/8/2013		frye	Lynn	carissa	Carissa Frye
10	1/9/2013		keiser	f	Colby	Colby Keiser
11						

Flash Fill will smartly fill a column based on the pattern of data it sees in the first column (it helps if the top row is a unique header row). For example, if the first column is all phone numbers that are formatted like "2125034111" and you want them to all look like "(212)-503-4111," start typing. By the second cell, Excel should recognize the pattern and display what it thinks you want. Just hit enter to use them.

This works with numbers, names, dates, etc. If the second cell doesn't give you an accurate range, type some more, the pattern might be hard to recognize. Then go to the Data tab and click the Flash Fill button.

5. Ctrl+Shift To Select

There are much faster ways to select a dataset than using the mouse and dragging the cursor, especially in a spreadsheet that could contain hundreds of thousands of rows or columns. Click in the first cell you want to select and hold down Ctrl+Shift, then hit either the down arrow to get all the data in the column below, the up arrow to get all the data above, or left or right arrow to get everything in the row (to the left or right, of course). Combine the directions, and you can get a whole column as well as everything in the rows on the left or right. It'll only select cells with data (even invisible data).

If you use Ctrl+Shift+End, the cursor will jump to the lowest right-hand cell with data, selecting everything in between, even blank cells. So if the cursor is in the upper-left cell (A1), that's everything.

Ctrl+Shift+* (the asterisk) might be faster, as it will select the whole contiguous data set of a cell, but will stop at blank cells.

6. Text To Columns

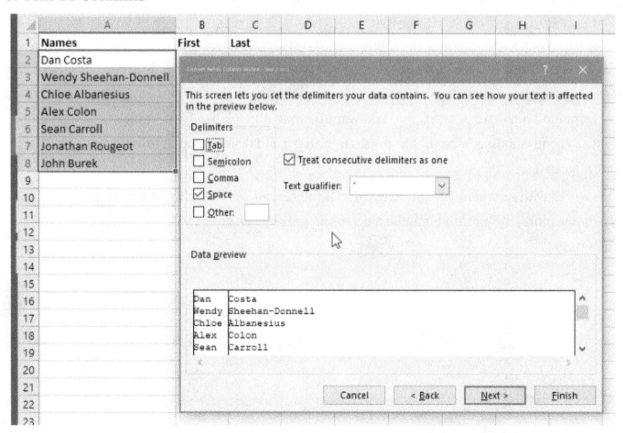

Say you've got a column full of names, first next to last, but you want two columns that break them out. Select the data, then on the Data tab (at the top) click Text to Columns. Choose to separate them by either delimiter (based on spaces or commas—great for CSV data values) or by a fixed width. Fixed width is utilized when all the data is crammed into the first column, but separated by a fixed number of spaces or periods. The rest is like magic, with extra options for certain numbers.

7. Paste Special To Transpose

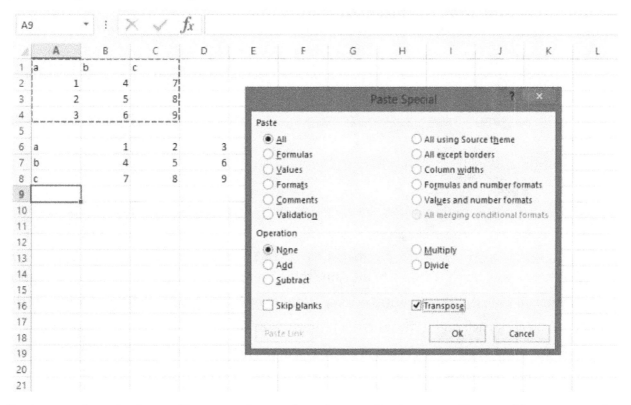

You've got a bunch of rows. You want them to be columns. Or vice versa. You would go nuts moving things cell by cell. Copy that data, select Paste Special, check the Transpose box and click OK to paste into a different orientation. Columns become rows, rows become columns.

8. Multiple Cells, Same Data

| B9 | ▾ | ⋮ | ✕ ✓ *fx* | Dan |

◢	A	B	C	D	E	F	G	H
1								
2		Dan		Dan				
3								
4		Dan		Dan				
5					Dan			
6			Dan					
7					Dan			
8								
9		Dan			Dan			
10								
11								
12								

For some reason, you may have to write the same thing over and over again in cells in a worksheet. That's excruciating. Just click the entire set of cells, either by dragging your cursor or by holding the Ctrl key as you click each one. Type it on the last cell, then hit Ctrl+Enter (not Enter alone), what you typed goes into each cell selected. This also works with formulas and will change the cell references to work with whatever row/column the other cells are in.

9. Paste Special With Formulas

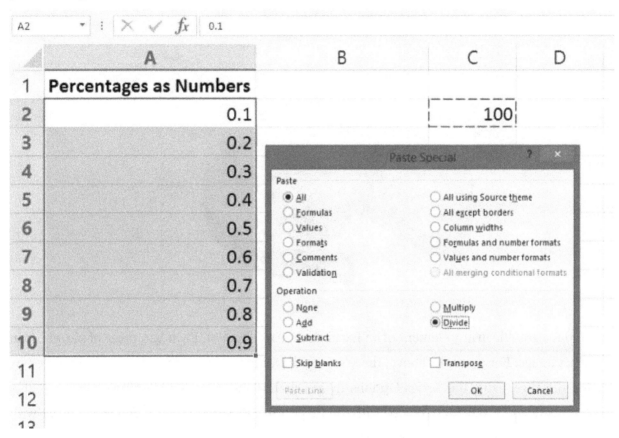

Let's say you've got a huge amount of numbers in the decimal format you want to show as percentages. The problem is, that numeral 1 shouldn't be 100%, but that's what Excel gives you if you just click the Percent Style button (or hit Ctrl-Shift-%).

You want that 1 to be 1%. So you have to divide it by 100. That's where Paste Special comes in.

First, type 100 in a cell and copy it. Then, select all the numbers you want to be reformatted, select Paste Special, click the "Divide" radio button, and boom goes the dynamite: you've got numbers converted to percentages. This also works to instantly add, subtract, or multiply numbers.

10. Use Graphics In Charts

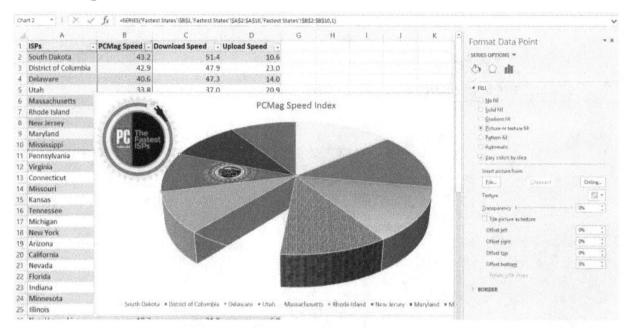

You can put a graphic in any element of an Excel chart. Any element. Each bar, piece of pie, etc., can support its image. For example, above, there's a South Dakota state flag on the pie chart (placed by selecting the slice, using the Series Options fly-out menu, and selecting "Picture or texture fill"), plus an embedded PCMag logo (placed with the Insert tab's Pictures button). You can even go with "no fill" at all, which caused that missing slice.

Clip art can be cut and pasted to an element, dollar bills to show dollars spent, water drips for plumbing costs, that kind of thing. Mixing and matching too many graphical elements makes it impossible to read, but the options you have are worth some digital tinkering. Let your resident graphic designer check them out before you use them.

11. Save Charts As Templates

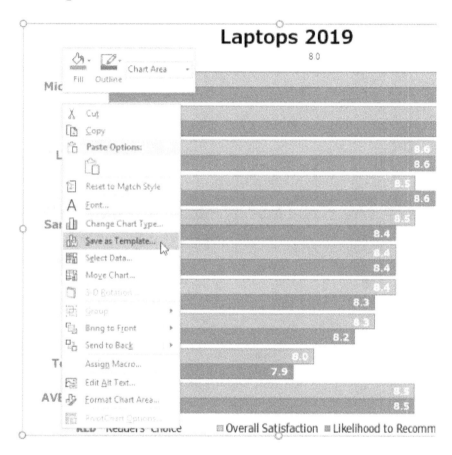

Excel has more types of charts than Jimmy Carter's got peanuts, but it's almost impossible to find a default chart perfect for your presentation. Thankfully, Excel's ability to customize all graphs is exemplary. But when you have to recreate one, that's a pain. It doesn't have to be. Save your original chart as a template.

Once a chart is perfected, right-click on it. Select Save as Template. Save a file with a CRTX extension in your default Microsoft Excel Templates folder. Once done, applying the template is cake. Select the data you want to chat with, go to the Insert tab, click Recommended Charts, and then the All Charts tab, and the Templates folder. In the My Templates box, pick the one to apply, then click OK.

Some elements, like the actual text in the legends and titles, won't translate unless they're part of the data selected. You will get all the font and color selections, embedded graphics, even the series options (like a drop shadow or glow around a chart element).

12. Work With Cells Across Sheets

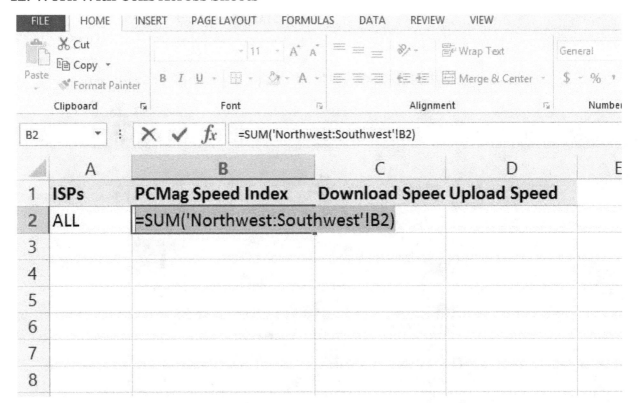

This one, called 3D Sum, works when you have multiple sheets in a workbook that all have the same basic layout, say quarterly or yearly statements. For example, in cell B3, you always have the dollar amount for the same corresponding week over time.

On a new worksheet in the workbook, go to a cell and type a formula like =sum('Y1:Y10'!B3). That indicates a SUM formula (adding things up) for all the sheets that are titled Y1 to Y10 (so 10 years' worth) and looking at cell B3 in each. The result will be the sum of all 10 years. It's a good way to make a master spreadsheet that refers back to ever-changing data.

13. Hide In Plain Sight

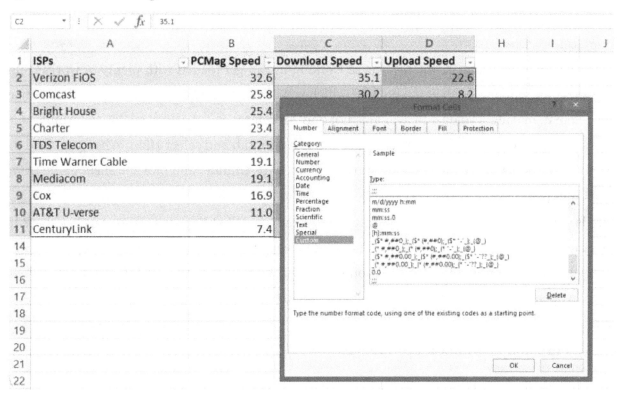

It's easy to hide a row or column, just select the whole thing by clicking the letter or number header, right-click, and select "Hide." (You can unhide by selecting the columns to either side all at once, right-clicking, and selecting "Unhide"). But what if you have just a little section of inconveniently placed data you want to hide, but still want to be able to work with? Easy. Highlight the cells, right-click, and choose Format Cells. On the Number tab at the top, go to Category and select "Custom." Type three semicolons (; ;) in the Type: field. Click OK. Now the numbers aren't visible, but you can still use them in formulas.

14. Hide A Whole Sheet

Your typical Excel workbook, the file you're working in can get loaded with plenty of worksheets (each sheet indicated by a tab at the bottom, which you can name). Hide a sheet if you want, rather than delete it, making its data still available not only for reference but also available to formulas on other sheets in the workbook. Right-click the bottom sheet tab and select Hide. When you need to find it again, you have to go to the View tab at the top, click Unhide, and pick the sheet name from the list that pops up.

There is also a Hide button on the View tab menu at the top. What happens when you click that? It hides the entire workbook you're using. It looks like you closed the file, but Excel keeps running. When you close the program, it'll ask if you want to save changes to the hidden workbook. When you go to open the file, Excel gives you what appears to be a blank workbook until you click Unhide again.

15. Use Personal Workbook For Macros

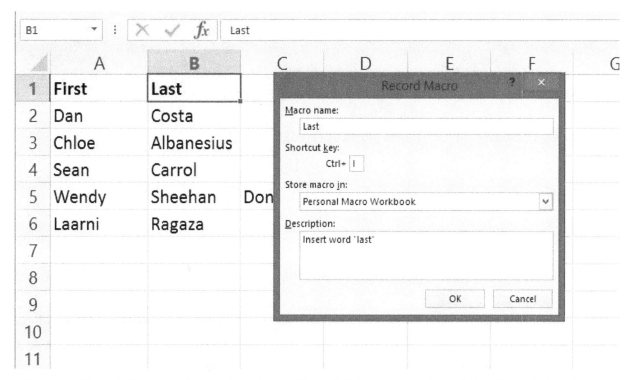

When you do unhide an entire workbook, you'll probably see a workbook listed you didn't know you hid: the Personal.XLSB file. This is the personal workbook Excel created for you; it's opened as a hidden workbook every time Excel starts. The reason to use it? Macros.

When you create a macro, it doesn't work across every single spreadsheet you create by default (like it does in Microsoft Word), a macro is tied to the workbook it was created in. However, if you store the macro in Personal. XLSB will be available all the time, in all your spreadsheet files.

The trick is, when you record the macro, in the "Store macro in" field, select "Personal Macro Workbook." (Record a macro by turning on the Developers tab, go to the File tab, select Options, click Customize Ribbon, then in the Main Tabs box, check Developers, click OK.)

16. Pivot! Pivot!

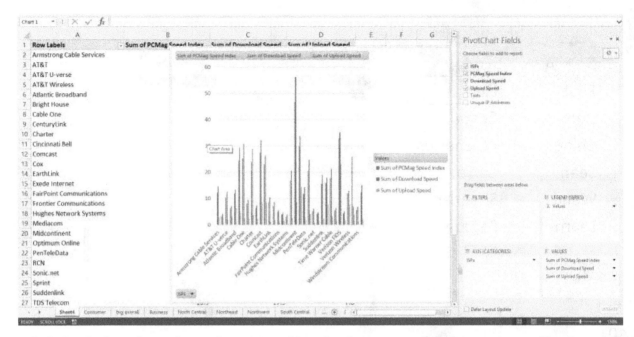

Whole books have been devoted to PivotTable. They're summaries of your giant collection of data that makes it much easier to parse the info based on your reference points. For example, if you've got the entire set of grades for all your students across all tests for the whole year, a PivotTable can help you narrow things down to one student for one month. It behooves anyone with big data to play with them (make a copy of the original data to play with first).

To create one, check that all the columns and rows are titled the way they should be, and then select PivotTable on the Insert tab. Better yet, try the Recommended PivotTables option to see if Excel can pick the right kind for you. Or try the PivotChart, which creates a PivotTable with an included graph to make it easier to understand.

17. Conditionally Format

	A	B	C		H
1	ISPs	PCMag Speed Ind⌄	Download Speed ⌄	Uploa	
2	Bright House	24.5	29.5		
3	Cable One	25.3	31.0		
4	Charter	24.0	29.0		
5	Comcast	27.5	32.3		
6	Cox	22.8	26.3		
7	Midcontinent	46.8	56.3	8.6	
8	Optimum Online	30.0	33.8	14.4	
9	RCN	20.6	24.7	4.1	
10	Verizon FiOS	32.8	35.2	23.3	
11	Wave Broadband	26.0	7.0	4.0	

Looking at a huge amount of data and wondering where the highlights are? Who has the highest (or lowest) score, what the top five are, etc.? Excel's Conditional Formatting will do everything from putting a border around the highlights to color-coding the entire table. It'll even build a graph into each cell so you can visualize the top and bottom of the range of numbers at a glance. (Above, the highest numbers are in speedy green, the lowest in halting red, with a spectrum in between.) Use the Highlighted Cells Rules sub-menu to create more rules to look for things, such as text that contains a certain string of words, recurring dates, duplicate values, etc. There's even a greater than/less than option so you can compare number changes.

18. Validate Data To Make Drop-Downs

	A	B	C	D	E	F
1					new mexico	
2		states			new jersey	
3			new mexico		new york	
4			new jersey		north dakota	
			new york			
5			north dakota		Penn	
			Penn			
6			mass		mass	
7						
8						

Creating a spreadsheet for others to use? If you want to create a drop-down menu of selections to use in particular cells (so they can't screw it up!), that's easy. Highlight the cell, go to the Data tab, and click Data Validation. Under "Allow:" select "List." Then in the "Source:" field, type a list, with commas between the options. Or, click the button next to the Source field and go back into the same sheet to select a data series—this is the best way to handle large lists. You can hide that data later, it'll still work. Data Validation is also a good way to restrict data entered—for example, give a date range, and people can't enter any dates before or after what you specify. You can even create the error message they'll see.

19. Screenshot Insertion

Excel makes it ultra-easy to take a screenshot of any other open program on your desktop and insert it into a worksheet. Just go to the Insert tab, select Screenshot, and you'll get a drop-down menu displaying a thumbnail of all the open programs. Pick one to insert the full-sized image. Resize it as you desire.

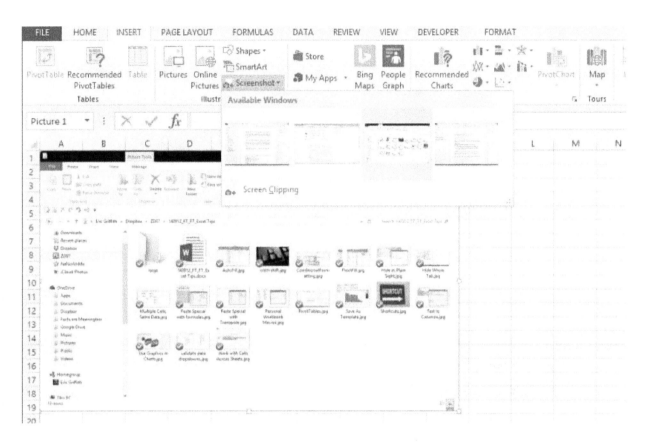

20. Insert Excel Data Into Word

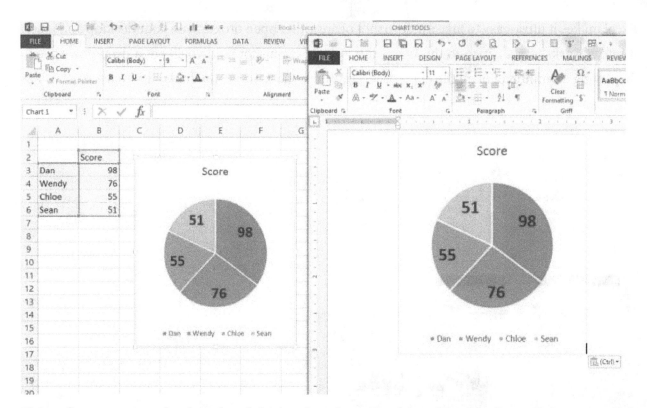

Thirty-five years ago, the thought of placing data from Excel into Word or PowerPoint was mind-blowing in the world of Office Suites. Today, there's nothing to it. Whether you're taking data cells or a full-blown graphical chart, copy and paste it into the other program. The thing to be aware of is, this is a link-and-embed process—if you change the data in the spreadsheet, it'll change in the Word DOC or PowerPoint PPT, too. If you don't want that, paste it as a graphic. Use Word's own Paste Special tool for that. Or, when taking it from Excel, go to the Home tab at the top, select the Copy menu, and use the Copy as Picture option. Then you can paste the graphic into any program at all.

21. Use $ To Prevent Shift

C3	▼ ⋮ ✕ ✓ *fx*	=(B3/$B$1)		

◢	A	B	C	D
1		100		
2		Score	Percentage	
3	Dan	98	=(B3/$B$1)	
4	Wendy	76	=(B4/$B$1)	
5	Chloe	55	=(B5/$B$1)	
6	Sean	=SUM(42,1,5)	=(B6/$B$1)	
7				
8		Score		
9				
10				
11				
12		48		

When you write a formula, you reference cells by their position, such as A1. If you copy a formula and paste it in the next cell down, Excel will shift that referenced cell, so it would say A2 instead. To prevent shifting, use the dollar sign ($). Type $A1 and cut and paste it to a new cell, for example, which prevents a shift in the column (A); A$1 prevents the shift in the row (1), and $A$1 prevents the shift change in any direction when copying a formula.

This is handy when you have a single cell to use in a whole bunch of formulas. Say you want to divide everything by 100. You could do a formula like =(A1/100), but that means you can't change the 100 easily across the board. Put the 100 in cell B1 and use =(A1/B1) but then when you cut and paste it down, it turns to =(A2/B2), then =(A3/B3), etc. The $ fixes that: =(A1/$B$1) can be cut and pasted down a row, but the $B$1 reference never changes. Then you can change the value of 100 in the cell as needed to experiment with other changes.

22. Perform Quick Analysis

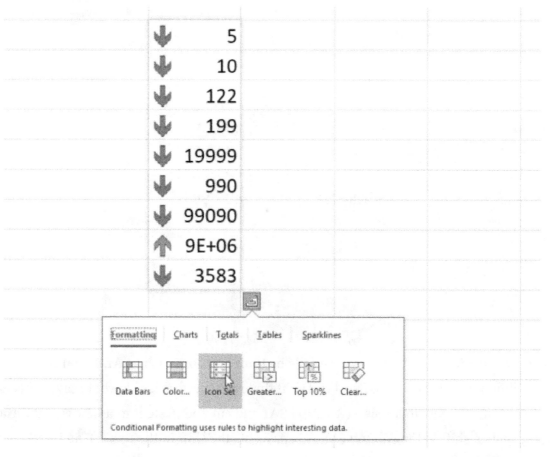

If you don't know exactly what info you'd like to apply to data in Excel, try the Quick Analysis menu to run through options quickly. Select the data and click on the Quick Analysis box that appears on the lower right. You'll get a menu that pops up with options to swiftly apply conditional formatting, create charts, handle totals, show sparklines, and more.

23. Quickly Add Without Formulas

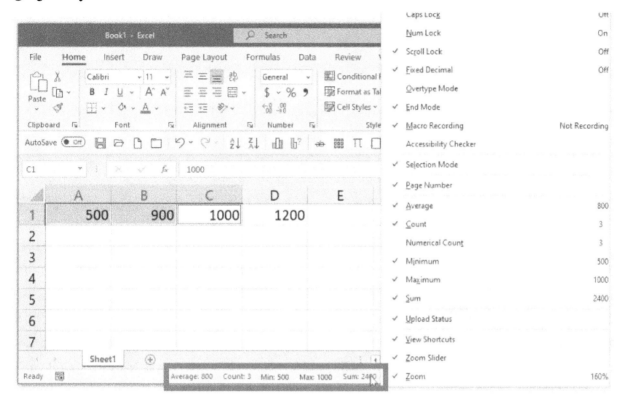

Got numbers in a spreadsheet you want a quick calculation on, without the hassle of going to a new cell and creating a SUM formula for the job? Excel now offers a quick way to do that. Click the first cell, hold down the Ctrl key, and click a second cell. Look at the status bar at the bottom and you'll see the sum of the cells calculated for you.

Keep your finger on Ctrl and click as many cells as you like, the status bar will continue to show the sum for all the cells. (Click a cell with letters/words as the content, it gets ignored.) Better yet, right-click the status bar to get the Customize Status Bar menu and you can choose to add other elements that can be quick-calculated like this, such as seeing the average or count of how many cells you clicked (or the numerical count, which is how many cells you clicked that have numbers).

24. Freeze Headers For Scrolling

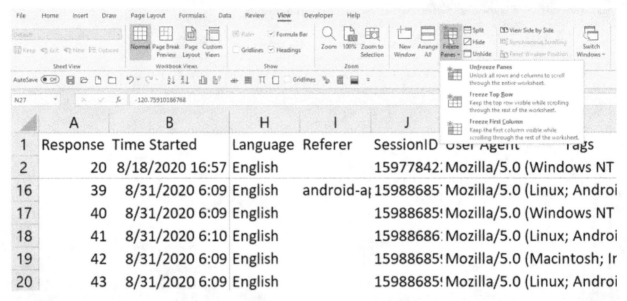

Working with a massive data set in a spreadsheet can be difficult, especially as you scroll up/down or left/right and the rows and columns may be hard to track. There's a simple trick for that if you've got a header row or column, where the first row/column has a descriptor. You freeze it so when you scroll, that row and/or column (or multiple rows and/or columns) don't move.

Go to the View tab and look for Freeze Panes. You can easily just freeze the top row (select Freeze Top Row) or the first column (select Freeze First Column). You can do both at once by clicking the cell at B2 and just selecting Freeze Panes. This is where it's fun, select any other cell and also Freeze all the panes above and left of it. Select cell C3 for example and the two rows above and two columns to the left won't scroll. You can see it in the screenshot above, indicated by the darkened grid lines. When you want to get rid of the freeze, you can just select Unfreeze Panes from the menu.

25. New Window For Second View

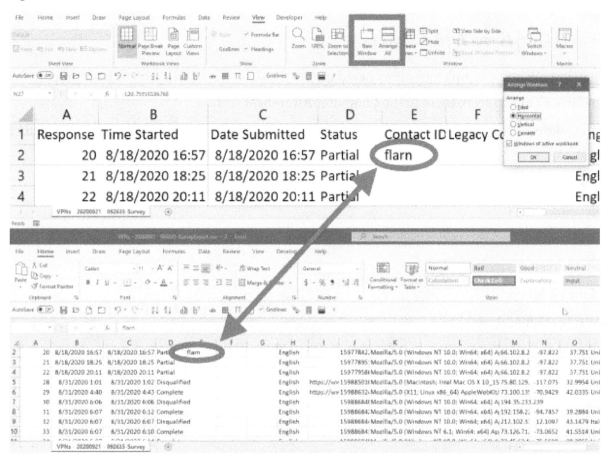

Spreadsheets can be enormous, and you may have to interact with different areas of the spreadsheet at what seems like the same time, such as cutting and pasting info from the top to the bottom over and over. If it's hundreds of thousands of cells, the scrolling that would take could make you nauseous. Or, you could just open a second window on your desktop with a view of the same spreadsheet. It's easy. In the View tab, click New Window. You can also click Arrange All to get them ordered on-screen in a way that works for you. You can see them Horizontally arranged above. Then, type something into a cell in one window, you can see it appear in the other window. This trick is especially handy if you've got dual monitors.

CHAPTER 12: MICROSOFT EXCEL QUESTIONS AND ANSWER

MS Excel Questions And Answers

Given below are a few sample questions based on MS Excel which will help candidates prepare for competitive exams to score more in the Computer Awareness section.

Q 1. The address that is obtained by the combination of the Row number and the Column alphabet is called _____.

1. Worksheet

2. Cell

3. Workbox

4. Cell Address

5. Column Address

Answer: (4) Cell Address

Q 2. Where is the option for page border given in the MS Excel spreadsheet?

1. Home

2. Insert

3. Format

4. View

5. Page Border cannot be added to excel worksheet

Answer: (5) Page Border cannot be added to excel worksheet

Q 3. Excel workbook is a collection of _____ and _____.

1. Worksheet and charts

2. Graphs and images

3. Sheets and images

4. Video and audio

5. None of the above

Answer: (1) Worksheet and charts

Q 4. What type of chart is useful for comparing values over categories?

1. Bar Graph

2. Column Chart

3. Pie Chart

4. Line Graph

5. Such charts cannot be created in Excel

Answer: (2) Column Chart

Q 5. There is an option to add comments in an Excel worksheet, what are the cells called in which comments can be added?

1. Cell Tip

2. Comment Tip

3. Smart Tip

4. Point Tip

5. Query Tip

Answer: (1) Cell Tip

Q 6. Which of the following symbols needs to be added to the formula bar, before adding a formula?

1. *

2. $

3. %

4. +

5. =

Answer: (5) =

Q 7. Which keyboard key is used for Help in MS Excel?

1. ctrl+H

2. F2

3. F1

4. shift+H

5. Alt+ctrl+home

Answer: (3) F1

Q 8. How can you activate a cell in MS Excel?

1. By clicking on it

2. By pressing the arrow keys

3. By pressing the Tab key

4. All of the above

5. None of the above

Answer: (4) All of the above

The questions given above are just for the candidate's reference and similar questions may be asked in the final exams. Aspirants can also get a detailed study plan at the Preparation Strategy for Competitive Exams page and based on it, can start their exam preparation.

A topic like MS Excel is important for everyone using computer devices to know and learn as it can be extremely useful in various fields.

One must understand the information given in this article as it will not only help with exam preparation but also help with a better understanding of how the program must be used.

Frequently Asked Questions On Basics Of MS Excel

Q 1. What is the definition of MS Excel?

Ans. MS Excel is a spreadsheet program where one can record data in the form of tables. This gives the user a more systematic display of data.

Q 2. What are the main features of Microsoft Excel?

Ans. The main features of MS Excel include inserting a pivot table, sorting tabulated data, adding formulas to the sheet, and calculating large data.

Q 3. What are the common MS Excel formulas?

Ans. Given below are the common calculations which can be done using MS Excel:

- Addition
- Subtraction
- Average
- Maximum and Minimum
- Concatenate
- Count

Q 4. What is a cell in Microsoft Excel?

Ans. MS Excel comprises a spreadsheet is in the form of a table comprising rows and columns. The rectangular box at the intersection point between rows and columns forms a cell.

Q 5. Can multiple sheets be added to a single spreadsheet?

Ans. Yes, MS Excel gives an option to add multiple worksheets to a single spreadsheet. The user can rename each of these worksheets as per their requirements.

CONCLUSION

Excel is the computer program created by Microsoft. For example, we can use these computer programs for analyzing data. EXCEL is specific of given the instructions and use for 3 Excel quizzes. Besides, Excel is a very fancy calculator and the most basic form. Microsoft Excel also helps us to control costs and easy to obtain the business information used for the value of the data. For instance, Microsoft Excel will become a tool for businesses and help them to make the most of their data. Microsoft Excel has become increasingly significant as it can be used for making the resources and return on investment. Excel is quickly and effectively to analyze and collate information.

In my opinion, Microsoft Excel 2010 is the most flexible and useful function for us. This is due to the reason that Excel 2010 can help us to build great charts. By using the formulas across the grid of cells can allow the businessmen to potential their data.

Furthermore, I learned how to use conditional formatting in the Excel 2010 include using different color shades, italics, and bolds. For example, we can via the Quick Analysis button select an appropriate coloring scheme.

Moreover, using Excel 2010 to identify trends is also the one I learned in Microsoft EXCEL 2010. For instance, it can help businesses to develop their future strategy. On top of that, Microsoft Excel can also help us to bring the data together from the documents and various files together such as insert tab or additional spreadsheets.

Besides, we can through the Excel Services to publish and share. For example, we can share business intelligence and sensitive business information with co-workers and business partners in a security-enhanced.

In the nutshell, online access also I learned from Excel 2010. Excel offers us used with the laptop, smartphone, and web-enabled PC for making mobile working viable and making remote.

Excel is a very flexible instrument to perform analyses and what-if scenarios. You use formulas in cells with one or more input cells to calculate the various situations. To ease working with different values and/or choices, you can put the controls from either the Control toolbox or the Forms toolbar to good use. Proper use of these controls makes your models easier to use.

The controls also enable you to ease data entry and at the same time improve data quality by minimizing the risk of wrong entries. For "day-to-day" use, I recommend the Forms controls. If there are specific options you need which are not offered by the form controls then you can also implement the Control toolbox (ActiveX) controls.

A spreadsheet as a collection of information distributed in columns and rows enhances the possibility of making calculations in a faster and more accurate way. Numbers, text, and formulas can be put together and presented in a fancy and attractive manner so it could be easy to understand the meaning behind the numbers.

The efficiency of Microsoft Excel depends on what kind of task you intend to perform on this tool. In a nutshell, at what level do you want to use it. If your purpose is limited to its basic use, MS Excel is a go-to application. However, if you are an accounting professional, you may need to look for its replacement. Should you decide the rest by understanding the pros and cons of MS Excel for business and learning.

Charts are a powerful way of graphically visualizing your data. Excel has many types of charts that you can use depending on your needs. Conditional formatting is also another power formatting feature of Excel that helps us easily see the data that meets a specified condition.